# The Toy Factory

*A Sammy & Brian Mystery #10*

By Ken Munro

Gaslight Publishers

*The Toy Factory*

*Gaslight Publishers*
*P. O. Box 258*
*Bird-in-Hand, PA 17505*

*E-mail: sammybrian@desupernet.net*

Library of Congress Number: 99-85809
International Standard Book Number: 1-883294-98-3

*Printed 2000 by*
Masthof Press
*220 Mill Road*
*Morgantown, PA 19543-9701*

# DEDICATION

*This book is for*
*Jonathan Chen,*
*winner of the Barnes & Noble*
*Sammy & Brian contest.*

*Special thanks to:*
*Det. Sgt. E. J. Abel*
*John Moore*
*Tracy Moore*
*Linda Baker*
*and Sandy Weidel*

# Chapter One

With some difficulty, the two men lugged the big brown bear from the pickup truck and propped it against the brick wall. Timing was critical, and the plan was right on schedule. They knocked on the nearby door, raced to the truck, and drove off.

The bear had been abandoned.

At least it had a wall to lean against, a wall that was part of a large brick building. The sign above the door read: Eckman Electronic Toy Factory.

The man who answered the knock on the door was dressed in work clothes. His name tag said, Elmer "Elmo" Fox - CUSTODIAN. Sticking his head out, he looked in both directions. When he saw the bear, his arm and leg muscles automatically started a retreat back inside the building. It took several seconds for his mind to replay the image of the bear. Elmer then realized that what he'd seen was a man-size, stuffed teddy bear.

Finally, leaving the safety of the doorway, the custodian ventured slowly toward the bear. It was the note and card dangling from the bear's neck that caught Elmer's attention:

*To: Greg Eckman*
*Hi, my name is Bigmoore.*
*I'm one of John Moore's bears.*
*Tomorrow is John's birthday. Some of his friends are passing me around the area so that important people like yourself can sign the attached Happy Birthday card. As you can see, the mayor of Lancaster and the police chief have already signed it. Please add your name to the list and put me outside tomorrow morning. Someone will pick me up. Thank you.*

The custodian frowned and scratched his head. He backtracked to the door and yelled, "Hey, Harry, come give me a hand. We have a visitor."

After some chuckles and head shaking, the two custodians tugged and pulled the bulky creature through the door and into the main office.

The time was six-fifteen. The factory's work force and management had gone home at five o'clock. The place was empty except for Elmer and Harry. They still had several more hours of cleaning to do.

At nine o'clock, they, too, were gone.

And the bear was all alone.

# CHAPTER TWO

Nothing that his best friend did ever surprised Sammy Wilson. So when Brian Helm burst into the bedroom, he didn't bother to look up from the computer. He could visualize Brian, short, with wavy brown hair and hazel eyes, sitting down and flopping back on the bed. But the loud crash that brought Brian's entrance to a halt caused Sammy to stand and survey the damage.

Brian meant to land on the bed. But instead, he tripped over his own feet and stumbled across the room. He missed the bed by two feet, slammed into the wall, and landed on the floor. He painfully unwrapped himself, rolled onto his back, and placed his hands behind his head. He glanced up at Sammy and said, "Hi. I bet you expected me to just walk in and sit quietly on the bed."

Sammy shook his head and pointed a finger at his partner. "You're not going to tell me you did that on purpose."

"Hey, I don't want to be too predictable. People get into a rut, doing the same things over and over. Well, not me. I do the unexpected. I surprised you, didn't I?"

"To tell you the truth, Brian . . ."

Brian didn't wait for an answer. Instead, he struggled to his feet. "Hey, I almost forgot. I have great news for you. Guess what? Joyce thinks she saw Bigmoore."

It took a few minutes for the name "Bigmoore" to register. Several doors away from Sammy's house was a shop that sold teddy bears. Moore Bears. Three days before, someone unbolted the two wire cables that secured Bigmoore to the wall in front of the shop. The life-size teddy bear had been a fixture in front of the shop for years. Each month the bear was dressed differently, according to the theme of the month. That month it was wearing a bathing suit and sunglasses.

"Joyce saw John Moore's bear?" asked Sammy. "The one that was stolen, and we promised to find it for him?"

"Yep, well, she thinks she saw it," answered Brian.

"Where did she see it?"

"Outside the Eckman Electronic Toy Factory."

"What makes Joyce think it's the missing bear? Was it wearing a bathing suit and sunglasses, and holding a sandbucket?"

Brian spread his hands apart with the palms up. "No, but how many six-foot teddy bears are there?" He shook a finger at Sammy. "And she saw two men unload it from a truck. They put it near the factory entrance, knocked on the door, and then drove away."

Sammy leaned back against the desk and smacked his lips together. "So we have a six-foot bear delivered to a toy factory, and Joyce thinks it's the missing bear. Is that it?"

"Well, not exactly." Brian ran a finger across his stomach and chest. "She also saw two faint line impressions going around the bear's body. Like maybe they were made by wire cables."

Sammy's face brightened as he bounced away from the desk. "Good old Joyce. She doesn't miss a clue." He glanced at the empty rocking chair that Joyce occupied when she worked a case with them. He looked again at Brian. "When did this happen?"

"Around six last night. She feels we should investigate it."

"Where's Joyce now?"

"She's outside waiting for us."

Sammy moved to the window and looked down. Across the street a camera was aimed at the window. Behind the camera was Joyce Myers, waving as she straddled her bike.

Joyce was the same age as the boys, fifteen. Her short brown hair framed an oval face with large hazel eyes. She wore a T-shirt and jeans. Like Sammy, she was a member of the Brainteasers Club at school. She had her own darkroom where she developed and printed her photographs. Because of her intelligence and photography and writing skills, she was called upon to help the boys with some of their cases.

Sammy's straight, dark hair spilled across his sparkling blue eyes as he spied Joyce behind the zoom lens. His face projected an inquisitive attitude. The hint of a smile indicated the potential of a new adventure.

Joyce Myers waved again.

Sammy waved back and made a thumbs-up sign with his fingers. He and Brian then hurried downstairs where he made a quick phone call. John Moore confirmed that Bigmoore, the bear, was still missing. The boys grabbed their bicycles and crossed the street to join Joyce.

The Eckman Electronic Toy Factory was located beside a new industrial development area one mile west of the village of Bird-in-Hand. It was set a half mile back from Route 340, known as the Old Philadelphia Pike. The eighty-year-old brick building was an eyesore compared to the large, monument-like office buildings recently built on precious farmland nearby.

Lancaster Farmland Trust, a local non-profit organization, worked hard to preserve and protect the rapidly disappearing farmland in Lancaster

County. With grants and the money it raised through contributions, the Trust bought the developmental rights to the farmland from the farmer. That meant anyone who purchased the land had to use it for farming.

The Barnside Industrial Park was one farm that got away.

"Joyce, why were you here yesterday?" asked Sammy as they neared the factory.

"You know my father's in real estate. I'm his official photographer," said Joyce proudly. She pointed down the road. "See that farm beyond the toy factory? It's up for sale. I took pictures of it yesterday for my father."

"So you saw the bear when you drove past the factory," said Sammy.

"Right," answered Joyce. Her eyes returned to the old building. "My father said this was originally a shoe factory. Then when cheaper shoes, made in other countries, flooded the market, it went bankrupt."

"After that it became Martin Toys," said Brian.

Sammy looked up at the sign and said, "And now it's Eckman Electronic Toy Factory." He shook his head. "I wonder what it will be two years from now?"

As the old building loomed before them, Joyce had second thoughts about the ownership of the big bear. Maybe the bear was made there at the factory. After all, the life-size bears have to be made somewhere. Maybe the lines going across the front of the bear were stitch marks. She would feel foolish if it wasn't John Moore's bear that she had seen.

Brian picked up speed and rode past Sammy and Joyce. He shouted, "It doesn't look like much. I can't believe anybody would produce electronic toys in an old run-down building."

The overcast August day and the dark clump of trees that wrapped itself around the back and sides of the old structure gave it an eerie, mysterious look. Most of the windows were boarded up and painted. The parking lot that normally held one hundred cars was only half full. Weeds were growing from the cracks in the macadam.

The day was hot and muggy, but a cold shiver exploded throughout Brian's body. He turned his bike and retreated to the rear of the bicycle convoy.

Because of the reflection from one window, the super sleuths couldn't detect the eyes that watched them from the second floor of the building. "Ah, I see I have company," said the figure sitting behind the desk. He turned his head and glanced down at the object in his hand. His face was rigid as the eyes returned again to the teens below. "I am ready if you are," said Mr. Smarty Pants.

# Chapter Three

The reception area, inside the entrance, was not what the teens expected. The room was empty except for neatly stacked boxes, catalogs, and posters, displaying the current line of toys. No one else was in the room. A nameplate on the desk identified the missing receptionist as Molly Day. A little brass bell nearby displayed a sign that read, Please ring for service.

Joyce stepped forward and tapped the bell several times. "The class will now come to order," she said in a whisper.

"All right, I'll order one of those and two of these," replied Brian, pointing to two toy boxes.

Sammy cringed and shook his head. Before he could say anything, a woman appeared from the next room.

From the stern expression on Molly's face, she didn't appreciate the teenagers' attempt at humor. She was in her mid-forties, tall, thin, and wore a long drab dress. Her dark, disheveled hair was clipped back carelessly with a cheap tortoise-shell barrette. Her face was plain and drawn, not unlike the pioneer women of the past. She wasn't exactly ugly, but Brian now understood why the Conestoga covered wagons were covered.

"Yes, what do you want?" she asked, giving the impression that she didn't want to be bothered.

Brian was ready to head for the door. She was hardly the kind of charming person he expected to find in a toy factory.

"We would like to speak to the owner or manager, please," said Sammy.

"Mr. Eckman is the owner. If you want to buy toys, we don't sell directly to the public. We only sell to wholesalers over the Internet. If you're here for a tour, we don't give them. Anderson Pretzel Bakery down the road gives tours."

The automatic rendering of words made Joyce believe Molly had the speech memorized.

"No," said Sammy, "we want to talk to Mr. Eckman about a large teddy bear that was left here yesterday."

Molly froze. Then without saying a word, she retreated to the office door and disappeared inside. Muffled voices were heard. When Molly reappeared at the door, she produced a half-smile. "Come on in. Sit down. Greg . . . er, Mr. Eckman will be here in a minute." Molly's face hardened when she eyed Joyce's camera. "You're not allowed to take pictures here, you know." She closed the door behind her.

The office was cluttered with paperwork, catalogs, and stacks of files. In one corner a curled, thread-like, white fiber dusted the floor. It reminded Sammy of cotton candy. A side worktable supported a computer system. Crumpled pieces of paper decorated the floor around the trash can. Evidently Mr. Eckman was a bad shot. On the front edge of the metal desk, among the disorder, was a cute, cuddly stuffed dog. It stood twelve inches tall and was a brownish yellow. The tag said her name was Honey.

Before Brian sat on one of the metal gray chairs with padded seats, he picked up the stuffed toy. He gave it a quick examination. "Hm, I don't see anything special about this."

"Put it back," whispered Joyce. "You shouldn't touch it."

"Brian, sit down," said Sammy, who was already seated.

When Brian tried to say good-bye to Honey by shaking her paw, the right-front leg fell off.

"Oh, you broke my leg," said the dog.

Brian's breathing increased. His face got red. His hands fumbled as he tried to reattach the leg by pushing it back on. When he applied pressure, the two hind legs dropped off.

"Now you've done it," said the dog. "I'll never be able to walk again."

By that time, Sammy knew what was so "special" about the toy. His attention was now centered on his friend, who was trying to make sense of it all.

Brian, bewildered and sorry he had picked up the dog in the first place, dropped it back onto the desk—and the head fell off!

Brian stared at the head, wondering what the dog was going to say this time. But the dog said nothing. The somber moment caused Brian to stagger back and collapse into the chair beside Joyce. He glanced again at the dog parts scattered over the desk.

Suddenly the dog's head began to wobble. "You didn't expect me talk with my head off did you?"

Sammy and Joyce burst out laughing. Brian, still in shock, managed a fake, "Ha, ha."

And then as if on cue, Greg Eckman walked into the room. Apparently this was a frequent ritual when visitors arrived. Mr. Eckman would vacate his office and wait for human nature to take over. Who could resist picking up a cute fluffy dog like Honey?

Greg Eckman, forty-five, was large and bulky and looked more like a wrestler than a businessman. His dark hair was full and combed straight back. His round face sported a mustache. A small cut with dried blood showed the results of a fast shave that morning. His suit coat was draped over the back of the desk chair. The tie missing from his open-collar dress shirt lay curled on the desk.

Brian stammered, "I'm sorry about the dog. I . . ."

A roar of a laugh barreled from Greg Eckman. He picked up the dog's head and placed it near his lips, and in a childish voice said, "Honey is cute, isn't she? Yes, you are the cutest thing." He planted a kiss on Honey's head and returned it to the desk. "She usually goes to pieces when we have visitors." Another explosion of laughter followed. He was still shaking as he lowered himself into his chair.

But the mood changed quickly. With hands folded on his desk and a grim look on his face, Greg Eckman, owner of Eckman Electronic Toy Factory, was all business. "Now, what can I do for you?" he bellowed. He looked at the camera hanging at Joyce's side. "You can't take pictures here."

Sammy was not frightened by Eckman's words. "We're checking on a large bear that was left outside your door yesterday at six o'clock."

"Why are you interested in the bear?" asked Eckman.

"John Moore, who has the teddy bear shop here in Bird-in-Hand, had a big bear stolen from the front of his store," said Sammy.

Joyce Myers moved closer to the desk. "I saw two men put a bear just like it outside this building."

Sammy did not miss the flush face and the rise and fall of Eckman's Adam's apple.

"I don't know anything about it," said Eckman finally.

"The bear was at your door yesterday," said Sammy without taking his eyes off Eckman. "It's not there now. And you say you don't know anything about it."

Mr. Eckman frowned and threw his hands in the air. "That's right. I never saw the bear."

Sammy jumped up and grabbed Brian and Joyce. "Then we'll have to go to the police," he said as he pushed them toward the door.

Greg Eckman flew up from the desk. "Who are you kids anyway?"

Sammy pointed to his two friends. "This is Joyce Myers, this is Brian Helm, I'm—"

"Sammy Wilson," said Mr. Eckman. He rounded his desk and raised his hand. "You're the three local amateur detectives who help the police. Oh, I think you're great." He shook their hands. "Yes, I read about you in the newspapers and saw you on television." He motioned toward the chairs. "Sit down. Sit down."

Eckman appeared more relaxed as he sat on the edge of his desk. "Okay, I know about the bear. It was dropped off here yesterday like you said. But evidently they didn't let you in on the secret."

"What secret?" asked Brian.

"The bear wasn't stolen. It's being used to surprise John Moore on his birthday." Greg Eckman explained how he had found the bear in his office that morning and about the note and card attached to it. "So I signed my name to the card and several of us dragged the bear outside. Thirty minutes later the bear was gone."

Joyce nodded. "Probably taken to the next important person."

"Maybe we're on the list," said Brian, rising from his chair. "We better—"

The side door to the office burst open. "Sorry to break in, but you said you wanted to know right away. Well, it's working," said the man wearing a sport shirt, khakis, and a large smile. Andy Good was slim, in his mid-thirties, and had dark curls for which girls would give up their rock star posters. He beckoned to Eckman. "This you have to see."

Eckman leaped from his desk and started toward the door. "We're coming, Andy." He glanced back at the amateur detectives and waved his hand. "Well, come on. We're about to see the biggest toy sensation of the year."

# Chapter Four

Beyond the hallway, a flight of worn steps led to the second floor of the old building. The simple sign on the wooden door announced that they were about to enter the Research and Development Department.

When the door opened, it was like walking into a modern building. In contrast to the disheveled and cluttered appearance of the office, the second floor was clean and well organized. The smooth, plain walls were painted a light green. Wood and frosted glass partitioned the whole room into office cubicles. Light was abundant. Fluorescent tubing roamed the entire ceiling, supplying the much-needed illumination. Only one small window gave evidence of the outside world.

All the activity was centered on one cubicle. A group of coworkers parted to allow Greg Eckman, Andy Good, and the teens to enter. The office had a desk and workbench. Neatly stacked boxes containing computer chips, fasteners, and material were on shelves about the bench. An assortment of stuffed toys lined the back counter.

The man behind the desk was Dale Martin, head of Research and Development. He was in his forties, with straight sandy hair and brown eyes. He, like the other engineers, was dressed casually, T-shirt and khakis. "Sh! Don't move," said Dale. He held in his hand a fifteen-inch humanized toy fox. The fox, wearing a shirt, pants, and shoes, held a pen in his right hand.

All eyes focused on the toy fox as Dale placed him at a miniature desk, pushed a button on his back, and waited.

They all waited. Nothing happened.

Sammy worked his way closer.

Still nothing. Until . . .

"Now watch," said Dale. He waved at the fox.

The fox turned his head in the direction of Dale Martin. "Ah, I see I have company," said the fox. He glanced down at his hand holding the pen and resting on paper. "I'm ready if you are," he said.

Dale pressed the PAUSE button and glanced up at the three teenagers. "This is Mr. Smarty Pants. He's a special tutor. He teaches writing. As you just saw, he turns himself on when he detects motion. I waved my hand and he responded." Dale pointed to the window. "We have another like him, sitting there by the window. He talks when anyone arrives or leaves the building."

"But, how does he teach writing?" asked Brian.

"Come here. I'll show you. I just got the bugs worked out."

Sammy moved closer and stood next to the fox sitting at the little desk.

"You notice Mr. Smarty Pants is holding a pen. If you dictate a story to him, he will write the story. The paper on the desk is on a roll. As he writes and comes to the end of the line, the paper moves up one space and his hand returns to the left side. He will continue to write until you say, 'Stop.'"

"He's like a private secretary," said Sammy.

"Yes, only he's made for young children," said Dale, "children from five to nine years of age. You can set the controls so that he prints or writes cursive. I have him set for printing." He looked at Brian. "Go ahead. Tell him a story. Pretend you're five years old, and start your story with—Once upon a time." Dale pressed the PAUSE button again.

"I'm ready if you are," said Mr. Smarty Pants.

Brian was in his glory—a chance to perform before an audience. "Once upon a time a mean old monster was crying."

"Once upon a time a mean old monster was crying," said the electronic fox, and printed the words on the paper.

Everybody looked to see if the fox printed the words exactly. It had.

"The monster was crying because he had no friends," continued Brian.

"The monster was crying because he had no friends," repeated Mr. Smarty Pants. The printed words followed on the paper.

"'I have no friends because I am ugly,' said the monster," said Brian.

The electronic marvel repeated and printed the same. Even the punctuation marks were in place.

Brian shook his head. "How does he know what punctuation marks to use?" he asked.

"How does he know what punctuation marks to use?" said the fox.

Dale quickly pushed the PAUSE button.

"Whoops, sorry," said Brian.

"That's okay," said Dale. "To answer your question, we have programmed into the computer software the patterns of word usage and different sentence structures. Certain words in relation to other words form predictable patterns. The program reads these patterns and applies the necessary punctuation. Same thing with words that sound the same but are spelled differently. The program will look for the pattern and hopefully apply the correct spelling. However, Mr. Smarty Pants is not perfect. He will make errors. But right now we're concentrating on what he does right."

Sammy was very impressed with the demonstration. But the price of such a high-tech toy would be tremendous, he thought. Mr. Smarty

Pants was not going to be under every child's Christmas tree.

While Sammy was focusing on the marketing value of Mr. Smarty Pants, Joyce was looking at its educational value. "This is great," she said. "As the child says each part of his story, he or she can copy the letters as the fox prints them. The child is learning to form letters. The letters form words. The child learns the words because he knows what he just said to the fox. He wrote a story. He is an author."

"Exactly," said Dale Martin. "And think how delighted that little boy or girl will be when he or she hands the story to the mother and says, 'Look, Mom, I just wrote this story.' And how proud the child will be when the story is read back by the mother."

Greg Eckman rubbed his hands together. "Okay, I like what I see. How soon are we going to be ready to market this baby?"

Dale frowned. The other engineers returned to their own office cubicles, leaving Greg Eckman, Dale Martin, Andy Good, and the super sleuths.

"Oh, before we get into that," said Eckman, "I want you to meet three celebrities from our area. This is Sammy Wilson, Brian—"

Brian stood tall. "Helm, Brian Helm," he said in a deep voice.

"And this is Joyce Myers."

"Hello," said Joyce meekly.

Eckman continued. "These are the kids who help the police solve crimes."

Brian cringed at the word kids. He lost about two inches of height.

The head engineer of the department smiled and extended his hand. "Oh, yes, I've heard of you. I'm Dale Martin, and this is Andy Good, my assistant."

After the handshaking was finished, Dale Martin asked, "Are you working on a case? Is that why you're here?"

"No," said Sammy. "We thought we had a problem, but Mr. Eckman cleared it up for us."

"I know you kids can be quiet about what you just saw," said Eckman. "This is top secret. Only the people in this room know about Smarty Pants. We want to keep it that way. Don't even tell your parents."

The trio nodded.

"We understand," said Sammy, staring at Brian.

"Good. Andy, will you show our visitors back downstairs?" said Eckman. "Dale and I have some things to discuss."

"Hey, before you go," said Andy, reaching for a fluffy gray rabbit on the shelf, "this is for you." He handed the twelve-inch rabbit to Joyce.

The look given by Greg Eckman and Dale Martin indicated that Research and Development was not in the habit of giving away free samples. Dale's look of surprise turned into a smile as Joyce accepted the toy.

Andy Good looked at the boys. "I don't think you would want one of these. Would you?"

"No, thank you," said Sammy.

"Not for myself, but I do have a younger sister," said Brian, not wanting to lose out on a free gift.

Andy smiled and handed Brian a stuffed dog. "These are obsolete stuffed animals that we don't need."

Brian was sorry now that he didn't mention that he also had a younger brother.

When they arrived back on the first floor, Andy said, "Let me show you something." He opened a door off the hallway and allowed the young detectives to look into the room.

It was exactly like the Research and Development Department upstairs but without the wood and glass partitions. The room was spotless. Workers, who sat at clean work stations, were assembling electronic toys. At the end of the room were two doors, one marked Shipping—Receiving Department and the other marked Inventory.

The teens watched as the workers carefully attached and soldered wires to circuit boards that were then inserted into the stuffed toys. Each toy was pressed against a battery wire and tested for operational efficiency. If the toy checked out, it was laid carefully into a basket. When the basket was full, it was picked up and taken further down the line, where each electronically operated toy was boxed. From there it went into a storage area.

The activity at workstation number sixteen came to a stop. The employee noticed that the room was being watched from the doorway. The worker's eyes locked onto the teens, committing their features to memory. When the door closed and the observers were gone, the employee stood and headed for the restroom.

The worker dialed a cell phone.

"Danny Boy, we have a problem."

# *Chapter Five*

"Boy, you certainly can't tell a building by its eighty-year-old bricks," said Brian as the trio parked their bikes in the parking area behind Sammy's house.

"But you can tell a man by the toys he plays with," returned Joyce. She shook her head. "In his office, Mr. Eckman was like a little boy."

Sammy nodded. "But upstairs at the demonstration, he was all business."

"Money hungry, if you ask me," said Brian.

Joyce hugged her stuffed rabbit. "Andy Good and Dale Martin seemed nice though."

"Hey, I'll trade you my dog for the rabbit," said Brian, holding up the stuffed dog. "My sister loves rabbits."

"Yeah, and I bet you do, too," said Joyce. "Okay, I like dogs better anyway."

They exchanged animals and continued toward Sammy's house. Brian examined the rabbit to make sure it was of equal value to the dog.

"John Moore is in for two big surprises," said Sammy. "One, when he gets Bigmoore back, and two, a surprise birthday party."

Brian glanced at Sammy's house, hoping to see the bear waiting there for the super sleuths to sign the birthday card. He frowned. "No bear," he said.

"Brian," said Sammy, "no one is going to bring Bigmoore here at this time of day. Moore Bears is right up the street. If Mr. Moore saw his bear, then good-bye surprise."

"When is Mr. Moore's birthday?" asked Joyce.

"Maybe it's today, and the bear is back on the porch," said Brian. "And the birthday card is hanging from its neck."

"Let's go find out," said Sammy, leading the way. He turned to his left, passed his parents' shop, and continued the short trek to Moore Bears.

That part of Main Street, otherwise known as the Old Philadelphia Pike, Route 340, was filled with visitors. Tourists were everywhere. Tour buses mingled with RV's, pickups, cars, and Amish buggies. The buggies were in control. They set the pace. While some tourists had experienced "jet lag," now, in Lancaster County, they had entered the "Amish lag" zone. The tourists who adjusted to this slower, gentler frame of mind benefited the most from their visit to Amish Country.

Sammy frowned, Bigmoore, the bear, had not returned to the porch. If he had, tourists would be photographing each other, snuggling up to the big bear. The absence of the bear, however, didn't keep them from entering the teddy bear shop.

Once inside, the three teens mingled with the tourists. Teddy bears of all kinds and sizes were everywhere.

"That's the teddy bear I want, Daddy. Buy it for me," shouted an older girl as she pointed to a very expensive Steiff teddy bear made in Germany. The girl with long blond hair appeared to be about eighteen and looked like a bone-thin fashion model.

The middle-aged man with her checked the price tag. "That's too good of a teddy bear. I can't afford that." The man nudged the girl to another counter brimming with teddy bears. "Here are some nice bears."

The girl pointed back. "No, I want that one. That's the one I want." She wiped tears from her eyes.

The man looked around and saw that people were watching. He put his arms around the girl. "It's okay sweetheart. I'll buy it for you later."

The girl's face brightened. "Is that a promise, Daddy? Is that a promise?" she asked and waited until the man smiled and nodded.

"Oh, brother," whispered Brian to his friends. "What a spoiled brat."

Sammy elbowed Joyce and in a low voice asked, "Did you ever act like that to get what you wanted?"

"Yeah, when I was seven years old."

The pathetic mood of the moment was changed when Tracy Moore, John Moore's daughter, appeared. She was in her thirties, tall and slim with short blond hair. Her casual dress and sense of humor was capped with a business-like attitude. The amateur detectives were no strangers to Tracy. "Hello," she said. "Did you find Bigmoore yet?"

Sammy wasn't sure how to approach the subject of the missing bear. Was Tracy in on her father's birthday surprise? In fact, was it her idea? If not, Sammy wasn't about to spoil the fun by letting the cat out of the bag. "No, no," he said. "I . . . I have a bet with Brian. His birthday is September seventh. He said your father's birthday is the same day. I said it wasn't. Who's right?"

Tracy frowned at Brian. "Where did you get that idea, Brian?"

Brian was caught unprepared. "Well, well, a lot of important people were born on September seventh." He shrugged and looked at the floor.

Shifting her eyes back and forth between Sammy and Joyce, Tracy said, "My father's birthday is the same as another famous man, Abraham Lincoln—February the twelfth. That was six months ago."

# CHAPTER SIX

The porch shade gave them some protection from the hot August sun. But they had no protection from the shock they received from Tracy. The amateur detectives couldn't believe it. John Moore's birthday was February the twelfth. They stared at the spot vacated by Bigmoore. Had Mr. Eckman lied to them about the bear? Why?

"He lied to us. Mr. Eckman lied. Right, Sammy?" said Brian.

"But why? That's the question," said Sammy.

"We did threaten to go to the police," said Joyce. "Maybe that's why. He thought he could put us off until he got rid of the evidence."

Sammy shook his head. "If a company like Eckman Electronic Toy Factory wanted a six-foot teddy bear, they could buy one. Why steal Bigmoore? It doesn't make sense."

"So if he told us the truth," said Brian, "then he received the bear with the note. Why would someone want Mr. Eckman to believe it was Mr. Moore's birthday?"

"I have a thought," said Joyce. "Mr. Eckman was asked to sign the birthday card. Maybe someone wanted his signature."

"But why use the bear for that purpose?" asked Sammy. "I can think of easier ways to get his signature."

"Yeah," said Brian. "It must take at least two big guys to lift Bigmoore."

Joyce's attention was diverted to the door. "Hey, look who's coming," she said.

"Daddy" and "the brat" came out of the store empty-handed and entered the shop next door. Both stores shared the same porch. After a few seconds, "Daddy" reappeared outside and motioned to them.

"What's he want?" asked Brian.

"I don't know," said Sammy. "Go over and find out."

Brian, who would never turn down a chance to perform, slipped into his secret agent image. He gave a deep cough, stood tall, and said, "I'll just mosey over there and size him up. He probably wants us for a secret mission. I'll report back to you later if I survive this dangerous encounter."

"Oh, Brian," said Joyce, giving him a push. "Go see what he wants."

Sammy and Joyce watched Brian as he slinked across the porch. The man whispered something. They exchanged words and gestures, then turned to look at Sammy and Joyce.

"What's going on?" asked Joyce.

"We're about to find out," said Sammy as he watched Brian return and the man disappear back into the shop.

Brian looked glum. He had shed his secret agent facade. "I was right. He did want us for a secret mission."

"You're kidding," said Joyce.

"Nope. He wanted us to go in and shoplift the teddy bear his daughter wanted."

"And?" said Sammy.

"He said the bear's price was nine hundred dollars. If we got the bear for him, he'd give us five hundred dollars."

"Do we look like hoodlums or something?" asked Joyce.

"Well, we are hanging around in a group, looking like we have nothing better to do," said Sammy.

"What did you say to him?" asked Joyce.

"I said, no. Then he said he'd give us six hundred. I said no and walked away."

"I can't believe that," said Joyce, shaking her head. "What kind of example is he setting for his daughter?"

"Brian, why don't you go inside and tell Tracy about the man and his daughter," suggested Sammy. "That way she can be on the lookout for them."

When Brian returned from inside, a new wave of tourists hit the porch. The super sleuths moved to the sunny sidewalk. Being bombarded by strangers only added to the frustration the trio was feeling at the moment. But it was nothing compared to the bombshell about to explode.

"Hello," said a familiar voice from among the tourists. It was Linda Baker. She and her husband ran the Amish Country Crafts shop across the street next to the post office. They lived in the apartment above the shop. In fact, it was the same building that housed the Bird-in-Hand Country Store before Sammy's parents moved the business across the street.

Linda was fifty, slim, and a little over five feet tall. She wore jeans, a T-shirt, and sneakers. Her brown hair was straight; her dark eyes were locked on Joyce. "I saw you over here with your camera," said Linda. "I need a passport photo. Could you take one of me?"

"Sure," said Joyce as she pulled the camera strap from around her neck. She made a quick check of her surroundings. "I don't like the harsh sun." She pointed to a spot on the porch. "There. Stand over there. That way we'll have soft light and a plain background."

After Linda positioned herself, Joyce clicked off several close-ups. "When do you need these?" she asked.

"In a day or two," said Linda. "I must submit

the photo with my application. A friend is rushing it through for me so I can leave next Friday."

Joyce nodded.

"Hey, how about I take a picture of you three together?" asked Linda. "Bird-in-Hand's answer to Nancy Drew and the Hardy Boys."

"Yeah," said Brian, standing tall and displaying a stiff profile.

Joyce smiled, handed the camera to Linda, and explained what buttons to push. "Stand back so you can get us all in. Take three shots. That way we might get one with Brian's eyes open," said Joyce, laughing.

"You mean with his mouth closed," said Sammy as he reluctantly joined his two friends on the porch.

Linda backed up to the edge of the pavement, aimed, and snapped three pictures. "You were standing in Bigmoore's place," said Linda as she handed the camera back to Joyce.

"Hey," said Brian, "now that the bear's gone, maybe Mr. Moore will want us here to sign autographs for the tourists. And they can take pictures of us and . . ."

"I hate to say this, Brian, but Bigmoore is more famous than we are," said Sammy.

"You mean a stuffed bear is more famous than I am?" asked Brian. "But . . . but, he's not even here. A bear that's not here can't be more important than me."

"Than I," Joyce corrected.

"Yeah, you, too," added Brian.

"But Bigmoore will be back soon," said Linda.

The way Linda said it made Sammy believe that maybe the bear *was* being passed around with a birthday card attached. "Why do you say that?" asked Sammy, watching Linda's eyes.

"I think he's being repaired," said Linda.

"Why do you think that?" asked Sammy.

"When they loaded him into the trunk, I saw some stuffing falling out of him."

"You saw the thieves stealing Bigmoore?" asked Joyce.

Linda pointed across to her apartment above the shop. "I was looking out the window late that night." Her solemn expression turned to puzzlement. "But, Bigmoore wasn't stolen."

"How can you be sure he wasn't stolen?" asked Sammy.

"Because I saw John Moore helping the other men load the bear into the truck."

# *Chapter Seven*

The questions were bouncing off Sammy's bedroom walls.

"What do you think? Was the bear taken to the toy factory to be repaired?" asked Brian, lying across the foot of the bed. He held the stuffed rabbit straight up in the air and waved it back and forth. "Don't we have quilters around here who can stuff and sew a bear?" he added.

"Why didn't Mr. Eckman tell us the bear was brought to his factory for repair?" asked Joyce from her rocking chair. "Why lie to us? Brian, are you taking your rabbit for an airplane ride?"

Brian lowered the rabbit and tilted his head to look at Joyce. "Well, at least I'm entertaining the rabbit while you have your dog sitting next to your camera on the floor. Big whoopee!"

From behind his desk, Sammy directed the conversation back to the matter at hand. "Why would the two men leave the bear at the factory door, jump into the truck, and hurry away? Why not stay and help carry Bigmoore inside?"

"Maybe carrying a bear into a building wasn't part of their job description," snickered Brian.

A thought froze in Sammy's head. He stood and went to the rocker. In a soft, mysterious voice he said, "Unless the toy factory is doing a *special* job for Mr. Moore."

Joyce looked up into Sammy's blue eyes and brought the rocker to a stop. "Yeah," she said, "like installing computer hardware."

Brian snapped up into a sitting position on the bed. "Hey, they're turning Bigmoore into a Smarty Pants. Put him back on the porch and he moves and talks to the tourists. Boy, what a tourist attraction!"

"Before you get all excited," said Sammy, "we have to remember something. Mr. Moore was the first person to announce that the bear was stolen. He wouldn't do that if he was having Bigmoore modified with computer hardware."

"That's right," said Joyce. "And there's no way he would file a missing . . . ah, bear report."

"So, what are we saying here?" asked Brian. "Linda Baker either lied or only *thought* she saw Mr. Moore help the men with Bigmoore?"

Joyce settled back in the rocker. "Let's go with the theory that Mr. Moore helped load the bear, and the bear was dropped off at the toy factory to have work—"

Sammy interrupted. "*Two days later* the bear ended up at the factory. Why two days later?"

Brian swung the rabbit through the air. "Maybe they took it somewhere else to get it fixed, and it didn't work out," said Brian. "So Bigmoore ended up with Mr. Eckman at the factory."

Sammy shook his head and collapsed into his chair. "I still don't understand why Mr. Moore would report the bear missing if he had helped to make it disappear."

They sat in silence for a moment.

Finally, Joyce asked, "Was Mr. Moore helping to promote his own surprise birthday party?"

"Ah," said Sammy as he headed for the door, "let's see just how serious Mr. Moore was in reporting the bear missing. I'll be right back. I'm going to call our friend, Detective Ben Phillips, at the police station."

After Sammy left, Joyce leaned back in the rocker and wiggled until the cushions gave a little. She glanced at the ceiling. To have something to do until Sammy returned, she said, "Brian, you know you have a problem."

"Don't we all?" said Brian as he relaxed his arm and allowed the rabbit to dive-bomb at his face."

"Your friend, Larry, the spider, is jealous now that you have that rabbit," said Joyce.

Larry was the name used by Brian to identify any spider that crossed the ceiling or walls.

He hated spiders and relieved the anxiety by making jokes about "my spider friend, Larry."

Brian twitched and quickly scanned the ceiling. "How do you know Larry's jealous? He isn't even here." The rabbit made another loop-the-loop above Brian's head.

"He's probably crying in a corner somewhere," said Joyce sadly.

"This rabbit isn't even mine. It's my sister's rabbit," said Brian.

"Try telling that to Larry," said Joyce, continuing the playful banter.

"And anyway," said Brian, "spiders don't cry. It makes their webs wet. The flies wouldn't stick. They'd just slip off and fly away."

"That's right," continued Joyce, improvising as she went along. "So Larry won't have any flies to eat. He'll get thin and then sick and then die—just because of that rabbit, which you *allege* belongs to your sister."

"Oh, yeah?" said Brian.

"Yeah," said Joyce in a childish, mock anger.

Brian looked down and pointed. "Well, your dog just poo-pooed on your camera." He smiled and then laughed because of the look on Joyce's face.

Joyce looked down and finally laughed, too, because it couldn't be true.

Sammy's entrance into his bedroom was in slow motion. He was in deep thought. His vacant stare caused the laughter to stop.

"Well, what did Detective Phillips say?" asked Brian.

"He said that we weren't to worry about the bear," said Sammy in a dream-like state.

Joyce and Brian looked at each other.

"And that's it? Nothing else?" asked Joyce.

"That's all he said and hung up," said Sammy.

"Wow!" said Brian. "So something's up. Right, Sammy?"

Sammy didn't appreciate being on the outside of a conspiracy. He could accept the need for it, but to Sammy, a conspiracy was a puzzle to be solved. It was his kind of challenge, and he was ready. With the visits to the toy factory and Moore Bears, he had already collected enough pieces of the puzzle to commit himself to whatever was going on. He concentrated on the puzzle pieces—and then—

The sparkle in Sammy's blue eyes told Brian and Joyce that a plan had been born.

"Can you both meet me at Moore Bears tomorrow morning at ten o'clock?" asked Sammy.

Both nodded.

"Sure," replied Brian. "What's our plan of action, boss?"

Sammy smiled. "We're about to fluff some fur."

# *Chapter Eight*

The tourists saw the Amishman riding his scooter along Main Street. Some wondered if he was an actor dressed as Amish for the benefit of the tourist trade. He was not. Whether tourists were in season or not, life went on for the Amish. If the Amishman was bothered by all of the attention, he didn't show it. He plodded along on his scooter, a mode of transportation that was sufficient for his needs.

As the Amishman passed Moore Bears, he noted that Bigmoore, the bear, had not yet been returned. He waved back at the two boys and the girl who were standing on the porch.

It was ten o'clock and the teen detectives were ready to face Mr. John Moore. Milly, one of the "bear keepers" in the teddy bear shop, sent the trio back to the office.

The man behind the desk was in his sixties, of medium build. His salt and pepper hair had a slight wave. He peered up through wire-rimmed glasses and quickly developed a smile. "Hi. This is a surprise—a visit to my office. Are you out chasing the bad guys who took Bigmoore?" He rose and shook their hands. "What can I do for you?"

Sammy was looking for signs of stress, guilt. Just how surprised was Mr. Moore to see them? The man's smile spread a little *too* far, thought Sammy. His words were *too* many.

"You were seen putting Bigmoore into the pickup, and we were at Mr. Eckman's toy factory yesterday," said Sammy with authority. "We know about the bear."

Sammy waited for a reaction.

The face would tell it all.

John Moore lost his smile. His cheerful attitude changed to one of concern and worry. He sat again behind his desk. He lowered his eyes and brushed his hand back over his hair. A muscle twitched in his right cheek as he said, "Look, I have to make a phone call. Can you come back later? We close at five. We can talk then."

"Sure," said Sammy. "We'll come back."

The super sleuths hustled back to Sammy's house and quickly claimed their brainstorming stations. Sammy sat behind the old, oak desk, Brian lay on the bed, and Joyce backed into the rocking chair.

She squirmed as she tried to adjust her body to the cushions. Not satisfied, Joyce stood and placed her hands on her hips. "This rocker hasn't felt right for the last couple of days. Somebody's been sitting in Joyce-bear's chair and it's all messed up," she said in a childish voice.

Looking at the ceiling, Brian pictured the last person who sat in the rocker. "You should be honored," said Brian to the ceiling. "A famous writer sat in that chair."

Mentally, Sammy was still locked in on their visit with Mr. Moore, but Brian's last comment wasn't missed. Sammy saw Joyce's blank expression. "Art Hansen, the writer from North Carolina."

Brian sprang up into a sitting position, sporting a large grin. "Remember our last case, The Tin Box? Art Hansen's writing a book about the missing college student." Brian pointed. "And he sat right there in your rocker."

"I'm impressed," said Joyce as she rearranged the cushions and tried another fitting. "Maybe when he returns for a book signing, he and I can sit down and share a bowl of porridge." She lifted her eyebrows and smiled as she and the rocking chair moved in agreement.

Brian relaxed back on the bed. Sammy watched as Joyce took the rocker through its paces, then allowed the rocker to coast on its own to a stop.

They each waited for the other to express his or her reaction to the short, puzzling confrontation with Mr. Moore. Finally, Sammy said, "My parents told me something last night about Mr. Moore." He paused. "At one time he attended the Lancaster Bible College."

Brian raised his head and Joyce squeezed the arms of the rocker.

Sammy leaned forward and rested his elbows on the desk. “He’s a member of the board. He’s a religious man.”

“But he lied about the bear,” said Brian.

Sammy nodded and continued. “My parents said, the people who work for Mr. Moore describe him as a wonderful, lovable, big teddy bear—with a heart of gold.” Sammy leaned back and took a deep breath. “Makes you wonder, doesn’t it?”

“He still lied about Bigmoore being stolen,” said Brian, resting his head back on the bed. “There’s something funny going on, and he’s part of it.”

Joyce nodded in agreement. “He said he had to make a phone call. Who do you think he called?”

“Probably Mr. Eckman at the toy factory,” said Sammy. “Whatever is going on, he’s getting things ready for his talk with us at five o’clock.”

“What *things*?” asked Brian.

“Yeah, and will it be the truth or more lies?” asked Joyce.

“I suspect it will be the truth,” answered Sammy. “You can only chew on a lie so long, then you have to spit it out. Guilt has a bitter taste.”

Joyce whipped out an imaginary notebook and pen and asked, “Can I quote you on that, Mr. Samuel Wilson?”

“Hey, I’ll give you a quote,” said Brian, his eyes roaming the ceiling. “There’s something rotten in Bird-in-Hand and it's not the birds. It's the bears, human or otherwise."

"That's already been said, Brian," proclaimed Joyce.

"Who? Tell me who," said Brian. "I want names."

"Shakespeare. And it was Denmark, not Bird-in-Hand," said Joyce.

Brian lifted his head. "If Shakespeare was here today, he'd say there's something rotten in Bird-in-Hand. That's definite." Brian produced a large grin. "And you can quote me on that."

Joyce broke the humorous mood by jumping from the rocker. "Oh, I almost forgot. I have more fuel for the fire. As I was riding my bike home yesterday, I had a feeling I was being followed. A blue Sentra sedan was behind me. It pulled to the side of the road, waited, then started out again, always staying behind me. When I got home, I ran into the house. I looked out the window, but the car was gone."

Brian sat up. "Just your imagination. Somebody was probably looking for a certain address."

"Well, how about this?" continued Joyce. "After supper I remembered I left my camera bag on my bike. When I went out to get it, the bag was open. My toy dog was still there but my camera was upside down with the strap hanging out of the bag."

"And the film?" asked Sammy.

"No film," replied Joyce.

"So they took the film," said Brian. "They thought you snapped pictures in the toy factory."

"No," said Joyce. "The camera was empty because I had already taken out the film."

"That is strange," said Sammy. "Did you take any pictures when we were in the factory?"

"No, I didn't," said Joyce. "Remember, the receptionist and Mr. Eckman said no pictures were allowed. I didn't want to get into trouble."

"But they didn't know that you didn't take any snapshots. Right, Sammy?" said Brian.

"That's true," said Sammy. "After we left the building, maybe somebody realized you could have used your camera during our visit."

Brian's hand pivoted on his side. "Yeah, like shooting from the hip. Click, click, click."

"What's 'the factory' afraid of?" asked Sammy. "Secrets being exposed?"

"Yeah," said Brian, "they're trying to protect Smarty Pants."

"I still can't rule out Bigmoore," said Joyce. "John Moore is involved in this somehow."

Sammy didn't say it aloud, but he wondered how dangerous their investigation was going to become. Then as an afterthought, he asked, "Did you develop the film yet?"

"Yeah, I did it last night. I have the prints down on my bike. I have Linda Baker's pictures I took and the ones she took of us. I'll run down and get them."

Joyce was back quickly with a bunch of eight-by-tens in one hand and the empty envelope in the other. She laid the pictures on the desk as she and Brian crowded around Sammy.

Sammy separated the top few photos. "Hey, these are too good to be passport pictures," said Sammy.

"The soft light and the plain background makes a pleasing photo," said Joyce.

"Plus the expert developing and printing you do in your darkroom," added Brian.

Joyce allowed the compliment to hang as she gathered up Linda's passport photos.

Sammy spread the remaining pictures across the desk. "These we can throw away," he kidded as he started to gather up the photos of the super sleuths, Sammy Wilson, Brian Helm, and Joyce Myers.

"No, you don't," said Joyce as she grabbed Sammy's arm. "I printed three copies of each, one set for each of us. Here." She handed three pictures to Brian, three to Sammy, and she picked up the third set for herself.

Sammy gave the photos a quick going-over and was about to place them into the drawer when something grabbed his attention. He raised the photo to his face. "Look at this picture. Do you see who's in the background?"

Both Joyce and Brian flipped through their photos until they had the copy Sammy was holding.

Joyce was the first to notice because Brian was peering at himself in the photo and thinking how "professional" he looked. "It's the man and his daughter who wanted us to steal the teddy bear," she said.

"What?" asked Brian, finally able to see other people in the photo beside himself. "Yeah, Mr. Money and his spoiled daughter."

"They're looking directly at the camera," said Sammy. "Notice the expression on their faces."

Joyce nodded. "Like they were caught in the act of being themselves, if you know what I mean," she said.

Still holding the picture, Sammy went to the window and pushed the curtain aside. Do you know what would be interesting?"

"No. What?" asked Brian.

Sammy gazed down at the traffic. "To find out whether they own a blue Sentra sedan."

# *Chapter Nine*

The three ambitious detectives sat on the stone wall that formed part of the parking area in front of the Bird-in-Hand Country Store. From there they watched the customers leave the Moore Bears shop.At five-fifteen, the last of the employees was gone.

The trio only knocked once and the door opened. Mr. Moore had apparently been waiting for them. As they entered the shop, John Moore lowered the front window shade. Semidarkness filled the room. He locked the door and led the teenage detectives back to his office. The teens looked at each other. Was Mr. Moore steering them into a trap?

Brian looked around, expecting to see Moore's accomplices in crime. "I can't stay too long. My parents are waiting for me outside," he said.

Sammy and Joyce glanced at each other. *It wasn't the dumbest thing Brian ever said*, thought Sammy.

"Come in and sit down," said Moore, entering the back office. He waited until the trio was seated then added. "We have a lot to tell you."

"We?" said Sammy.

Another door to the office opened. Daddy and his spoiled daughter entered!

Brian bolted for the other door. His chair slammed back against a table. Catalogs and books fell to the floor. One falling book hit a plastic dish and sent it sailing through the air. It hit Brian square in the back. He stopped, raised his hands, and yelled, "I give up! I give up!"

"Brian, if you put your hands down, we'll promise not to shoot," came a voice from a third person who entered the office.

Shaking, Brian slowly turned and joined Sammy and Joyce in examining the man with the familiar voice.

It was Detective Ben Phillips.

"What is this? What's going on?" asked Sammy. Never in his life had he been so unprepared for what was happening.

Detective Phillips smiled. It wasn't often Sammy and his friends were caught off guard. Finally he said, "Sammy, Brian, and Joyce, I want you to meet Agent Ted Manners, an FBI agent out of Philadelphia."

"Daddy" stepped forward and extended his hand. The three teens reluctantly shook his hand.

"And this," said Detective Phillips, pointing to the young woman, "is Julie Greenleaf."

"Spoiled Brat" shook hands. "I'm sorry we had to deceive you as we did," she said, immediately smashing her image as an eighteen-year-old brat. "I hope there are no hard feelings."

Brian flexed his back muscles. He wanted to say plenty about hard feelings but remained quiet.

"Julie Greenleaf was brought in as an aide to help us," said Manners. "She has certain skills that we needed in an emergency."

Sammy adjusted to the fact that the man was FBI and the girl his aide, but he wondered what the FBI connection was to Mr. Moore, the bear, and the factory, "But why us?" he finally asked.

Ted Manners took over. "We had a surveillance on the toy factory. We saw you three enter and we saw you exit. We had no idea at the time who you were. It wouldn't be the first time teenagers committed espionage. We needed to know whether you could be bought. When you entered Moore Bears, Julie and I quickly improvised our little act to test your morals. Were you law-abiding citizens? Did you have criminal tendencies? Were you one of them?"

"One of whom?" asked Joyce.

"Espionage? What espionage?" asked Brian.

Ted Manners ignored the questions and continued. "When Brian turned down the offer of five hundred dollars to shoplift the teddy bear, the next step was to check your police record. Needless to say, Detective Ben Phillips filled us in on your crime-solving ability and the mysteries you've unraveled. It seems you're local celebrities. Now that we know that you're the good guys, we could use your help."

"What exactly is going on here?" asked Sammy.

"It's a matter of national security," said Manners with a grim face. "It involves certain computer chips falling into the wrong hands. You've heard about the top secret missile guidance computer chips that ended up in China. Some scientists freely exchange ideas around the world. Sometimes secret data falls into the wrong hands. It's difficult to keep a lid on ideas. However, we investigate and prosecute when individuals deliberately pass classified information and technology into unauthorized hands."

"So this is about computer chips," said Sammy, "and the factory is involved."

Ted Manners nodded.

"You mean someone is trying to steal the secret to Smarty Pants?" asked Brian.

Sammy noticed that Julie Greenleaf smiled at Brian's comment. They knew what was happening inside the factory.

"It's more serious than that," said Manners. "It's top secret and involves national security. But I can tell you this. The computer chip in question entails the sending, receiving, and the decoding of sensitive intelligence information. Actually it's several chips containing software assembled as a module. It's code name is CRACKERJACK. It cracks codes and a guy named Jack developed it. Someone is trying to smuggle it into China."

"Where is CRACKERJACK produced?" asked Sammy.

"The modules are made for the United States government by Argus Solutions in California. Argus Solutions also just happens to be the company who supplies Eckman's toy factory with the chips it uses in its electronic toys. Last week we received word from an informant that a CRACKERJACK module was smuggled out of Argus Solutions in a shipment of computer chips to the toy factory. We now believe the module was sent to the toy factory because of the factory's shipping potential. They ship toys all over the world."

Sammy brushed his hair back from his eyes. "You're saying someone at Argus Solutions arranged with somebody at the toy factory to have the module sent to China concealed in a shipment of toys."

"That's the way we see it," said Manners.

"What does that have to do with the bear?" asked Brian.

"I'm getting to that. After the informant contacted us, we gained a warrant to search the Eckman Electronic Toy Factory. But we didn't want to tip our hand. We had to go in without Greg Eckman or his employees knowing we were there."

"Okay, so you have a search warrant," said Joyce. "But does the law allow you to search the factory without Mr. Eckman's knowledge?"

"Yes, when the security of our country is involved," Manners answered.

"And this is where Mr. Moore's bear comes in," said Sammy. "You used the bear to get you inside the factory."

Agent Manners patted John on the back. "Right. John and I have known each other for years," said Manners. "We grew up together and both attended the Milton Hershey School. Over the years we developed a friendship. Later, John became a businessman, and I was recruited by the government."

"Some friendship," teased John Moore. "What do you think of a friend who would make me lie about Bigmoore being stolen. When this is over, I'm going to write a book called *I Had to Lie for the FBI.*"

"Others have already written that book," said Manners. Then shifting into a serious mood, he said, "Your bear will be returned as good as new. Sammy, you said we used the bear to get inside the factory. How did you know?"

"When my friends and I were in Mr. Eckman's office, I saw polyester fiber on the floor. The kind that's stuffed into soft dolls and toys. The bear had been in the office overnight. And with what you said earlier, I remembered the story about the Trojan Horse."

"Ah, the Trojan Horse," said Agent Manners.

"Sure," said Joyce, following up on Sammy's disclosure, "like you, the Greeks wanted to get inside the walled city of Troy and conquer their enemy. In your case it's the toy factory. The Greeks built a giant, hollow wooden horse and hid warriors inside. You borrowed Bigmoore, the bear, and placed someone inside. That's why it took two days to deliver the bear to the factory," continued Joyce. "It took that long to modify the bear so someone who is small and thin could fit inside and breathe."

Sammy looked at Julie Greenleaf and pointed. "Someone like you, Miss Greenleaf."

Agent Manners nodded his head. "Julie Greenleaf is a computer hacker. She uses a computer like a burglar uses burglar tools. When she was in college, she managed to break into the school's main computer and manipulate her grades. She tried something similar with a bank. She was caught, put in jail, and as a result she came to our attention. We needed someone bold and small with computer skills. Miss Greenleaf was that person."

Julie, embarrassed, grinned and nodded. "They want me to join the FBI, so I'm thinking about it. Go on with your story, Joyce."

Joyce was intrigued by Julie's surprising background, but she managed to return to her story. "The Greeks placed the horse outside the walls of Troy. When the Greeks were gone, the

Trojans pulled the horse inside, thinking it was a gift. You left the bear at the factory door. The custodians dragged it inside, thinking it was part of a surprise birthday stunt for Mr. Moore. Later that night, Julie unzipped the bear, or whatever, and was free to investigate."

"Don't they have motion detectors inside the building?" asked Sammy.

"No, they only have alarms at the entrances to the building," said Manners. "We knew that beforehand. That's why Julie, once inside, could move about freely."

"My time was spent on the office computer," said Greenleaf. "First, I had to decode the password, which was easy. Most people use family names, birth dates, or telephone numbers as passwords. Agent Manners supplied me with a long list of possibilities. Once into the hard drive, I downloaded files."

Joyce frowned, shifted her body, and stared at Agent Manners. "Are you people allowed to just go into anyone's computer and read all the personal files?"

Julie answered, "I was told to access and download only the files that related to the case. I only copied the employee list, customer names and addresses, purchase orders, and shipping dates. I was to look for shipments headed for China."

Manners squeezed Julie's arm, indicating she need not say anymore. "Joyce, to answer your question, yes, we are allowed by law to do that. Especially when it involves the transfer of classified technology, such as CRACKERJACK. Eckman Electronic Toys has a web page," he said. "Most of their toys are sold wholesale online. The orders are packaged and shipped by UPS."

"Did you find any shipments going to China?" asked Brian.

"Yeah, one. It went out yesterday," said Manners. "The shipment was inspected this morning by customs." Agent Manners leaned against the wall and looked at the floor. "They found nothing." He glanced at Sammy and grimaced. "And this is where we differ from the Trojan Horse story. At night, when the city of Troy was asleep, the armed Greeks slipped out of the wooden horse and opened the gates. The waiting Greek soldiers stormed inside and conquered Troy. Well, we didn't find CRACKERJACK and capture the bad guys."

"Maybe you tipped your hand when you used the Trojan bear," said Sammy. "The module was to be in the shipment, but they were scared off."

"That's a possibility," said Manners. "Yesterday morning, after the bear containing Julie had been picked up, Eckman could have discovered someone had tampered with the computer."

Julie spoke up. "I'm very good at what I do. Eckman doesn't have a clue that I was there."

Detective Ben Phillips stepped forward. His impressive frame of six foot two, two hundred twenty pounds overpowered everyone in the room. This middle-aged detective with a receding hairline, thin mustache, and dark, piercing eyes had the trio's attention. "And now the FBI is asking for your help," he said. "For the security of our country, they must locate CRACKERJACK and identify the bad guys."

Brian tugged at his jeans and gave a cough. "Did you tell them about how we helped the United States Marshals at Kitchen Kettle Village in our case, Creep Frog?"

"Yes, he did," said Manners. "That's why the FBI wants to take another shot at the toy factory. We want to use you three to do it."

Sammy remembered how he and Brian had been "used" by the marshals. He wasn't about to jump into the same boat. He wanted to be ready this time. "How can we help?" he asked.

"We want you to act as a buffer zone between the FBI and the toy factory. You know the area, you know the people, and you're smart. CRACKERJACK will be shipped out sometime. When it is, we want the person responsible. You can help us catch him."

Brian was overwhelmed by what the agent said. "All by ourselves?" he asked.

"Oh, no. You'll have the FBI and the police as backup."

Sammy mentally formed an approach that he and his partners could use. He was about to learn if Manners' recruitment had strings attached. Would the super sleuths be puppets of the FBI or free to investigate on their own? Sammy had to know. He didn't like to be controlled by others.

"You don't look all that thrilled," said Manners. "Is something wrong?"

"No," said Sammy. "We'll help you if we can run our own investigation. I would like to suggest an approach we used in another case."

"Great, go ahead," said Manners.

"Joyce has written special features for the *Lancaster Sunday News*. What if we talked Mr. Eckman into allowing her to write an article about him and his electronic toy factory? It would be good public relations for him and his factory."

"That way she'll get to interview people and check out the place," said Manners.

"And I really will write an article for the paper," added Joyce.

"We'll try to go with her as protection," said Sammy.

"Great idea," said Manners, "*if* Greg Eckman buys the concept."

"It's worth a chance," said Sammy. "I'm sure Joyce can turn on her charm and lead Greg Eckman down the path of vanity and greed."

"I think Mr. Eckman already has that path worn out," said Brian.

"Hey, don't I get to do something in this buffer zone of yours?" asked John Moore.

Agent Manners patted Moore's shoulder. "Let's just say we'll keep you in reserve."

Moore smiled and nodded. "Oh, boy, I'm a reserve in the buffer zone."

The agent approached the teens. "Okay, now back to you three. Once in, you roam around, interview people, keep your eyes open, and maybe stumble onto something. The shipment came in through the Receiving Department. That's where I'd start. Interview whoever is in charge there. Find out where the parts go after they're unpacked. Who has access to the incoming shipments from Argus Solutions? That kind of thing."

Brian crossed his arms over his chest, stood tall, and took a deep breath. In his deepest voice, he said, "We narrow down the search until it leads to one person. Yep, we can handle that."

"It won't be easy," said Manners. "According to what Julie found in the computer, sixty-two people work there. Any one of them could have gotten their hands on the chip."

Sammy had one more piece of the puzzle to reexamine. He looked at Ted Manners and Julie Greenleaf. "Do either of you own a blue Sentra?"

"No, why?" asked Manners.

Sammy had Joyce tell of her experience the previous night and about the contents of the film.

When Joyce finished, Manners said, "You've rattled somebody's bones. And I'll tell you right now, it wasn't ours. My boss doesn't approve of sending you three back into that factory. But, Detective Phillips assured us of your skill and experience to pull this off." Then sounding like a father, he added, "So be careful."

"Today's Friday," said Phillips. "I assume you'll wait until Monday to return to the factory."

The teenage detectives looked at each other. "Joyce will start Monday as a reporter for the *Lancaster Sunday News*," said Sammy. "Brian and I will go along as friends."

"You better have a backup plan," said Manners, "in case Greg Eckman doesn't want to be written up in the newspaper."

"I already have one he might go for," said Sammy.

"And?" asked Manners.

"We'll offer Mr. Eckman a free photographic layout of himself and his factory."

# *Chapter Ten*

Greg Eckman hopped, skipped, and jumped around like an overgrown kid. The second phase of experimental testing of Smarty Pants had been successful. The computerized fox performed as expected. The mechanical operation proved efficient. After several more months of safety and endurance testing, Smarty Pants would be ready for mass production and distribution.

The cheery mood of the boss as he popped into the shipping and receiving room left Marty gaping. The only time the boss ever came to see him was to find fault or to complain about something.

"Marty Shipman, I want you to meet my three friends," said Eckman as he ushered the amateur detectives into the room. "This is Joyce Myers, Sammy Wilson, and Brian Helm. Joyce is writing a story for the local paper. Tell her what she needs to know about you and your department."

Marty was twenty-eight. His long blond hair spilled down from under a baseball cap. He was tall and lanky, his face pitted from an early illness. His khaki pants and shirt were wrinkled and dirty, characteristic of a person isolated in his own little world. Marty Shipman seemed more relaxed as he shook the teenagers' hands. "You look too young to be a reporter," he said.

"Don't let their age fool you," sang Eckman. "These are high-caliber kids who have many talents." He winked at the trio like a kid hiding a secret. "So take good care of them. Tell them what they want to know. But remember, I'm the one who hires and fires around here," he said with a pointed stare and a smile on his lips.

"I'll remember that, Mr. Eckman," said Marty.

"Oh, and if I'm not back in time," added Eckman, "they want to go to inventory next." With that, the boss hustled out the door.

Marty leaned back against his desk and spread his arms. "What we do here in this company is receive parts, assemble parts, box the finished product, and then ship it out. I'm in charge of the first step and the last step. I receive and I ship."

From what Marty said, Sammy figured the man was no dummy. His thoughts were organized, his words to the point. Sammy glanced at Joyce for clues that she might be thinking the same thing, but Joyce was busy making notes on what was being said and on her own observations.

"Is your last name really Shipman?" asked Brian.

"Sure, that's how I got this job," said Marty with a straight face.

"Yeah?" said Brian.

Joyce looked up. "He's only kidding," she said before Brian dug himself deeper into a hole.

"Do you ever have merchandise stolen?" asked Sammy.

"You mean because we receive and ship out valuable merchandise? Nope. I run a tight *ship* here," said Marty, grinning and looking at Brian.

Brian didn't bite.

Marty Shipman raised a finger. "I run this department by myself. I count and check off everything that comes into this place. See that stack of boxes? I just checked it in. The packing slip said six cartons and that's what's there. I get a computer printout of the orders going out." Marty walked the teens to a pile of neatly stacked boxes. "I check off all packages that go into the UPS truck." He dipped his finger up and down. No way anybody's going to heist anything from this department."

"Do you ever have shipments come in containing extra merchandise?" asked Sammy. He, Joyce, and Brian waited for Marty's reaction to the question.

"Look, whatever happens before the merchandise gets here, and what happens to it after it leaves, is not my responsibility."

The three investigators backed away from the employee.

Shipman saw their reaction. He relaxed and took a deep breath. "I'm sorry. Sure, sometimes there is an over shipment or a shortage. But that's the way it's received, as an overage or shortage."

Joyce patiently continued her note-taking on a large yellow tablet.

"So when a box of, say, computer parts comes in and it's marked—quantity 100, you open the box and count the pieces," said Sammy trying to lead Shipman to the truth.

"Well, no. If I receive two boxes marked one hundred pieces, I check in two boxes. It's up to the Inventory Department to open and count the contents of each box."

There it was. The Inventory Department opened the cartons. The trio looked at each other and smiled.

Joyce thought of her toy dog. "Are the stuffed toys made here or are they shipped in?"

"No, they're shipped in. The toys are made to our specifications in Taiwan. What we do here is insert the mechanical and electronic parts."

"Well, that's about it," said Joyce. She handed her notes to Brian and grabbed her camera. "Could I get a picture of you holding your clipboard over there by those packages?"

Marty shook his head. "You're not allowed to take . . . Oh, for the newspaper. Sure, wait till I comb my hair."

"No, you look great," said Joyce. "I want the public to see you in action, a man who's in charge."

Sammy bit his lip as he watched Joyce pose the employee at various locations around the room. After five shots, Joyce had the whole Shipping and Receiving Department on film.

Joseph Sweeney welcomed the "reporters" and made them feel at home. In his sixties, balding, and quite thin, he was not about to give the trio a whirlwind tour of the inventory room. His movements were slow and deliberate. They suited a man responsible for maintaining an accurate control of parts that lay in countless bins.

"Now tell me. What paper is this for?"

"The *Lancaster Sunday News*," said Joyce.

Joseph Sweeney's face lit up. "I get that at home. What do you want to know?"

"First, let me take your picture," said Joyce. She laid her notes on the desk and raised her camera. "Mr. Eckman said it's okay to take pictures for the story," said Joyce, seeing "factory policy" taking hold of Mr. Sweeney's body.

"Well, okay, if the boss said so," said Sweeney as he smiled and posed.

"Tell us what you do in this department," said Joyce, snapping pictures from different angles.

"I count the merchandise that comes in here." Sweeney swallowed and continued. "And I'm responsible for all the goods that leave this room." He shuffled to his desk and picked up a slip of paper. "When anyone in the Assembly Room or in R and D needs parts, they must fill out this order form and sign it."

Brian grinned. "R and D, that's Research and Development. Right, Mr. Sweeney?"

The man nodded slightly.

Joyce flipped a yellow page and kept writing.

"Are you saying that no one can take something from this room without an order form?" asked Sammy.

Joseph Sweeney executed another nod.

"This is very valuable inventory you have here," said Sammy. "When new shipments come in, what happens if the count is wrong?"

"I call in Mr. Eckman, and he verifies the overage or shortage."

Joyce kept writing.

Sammy didn't want to be responsible for giving the old man a heart attack, but he had to ask. "What if you discovered an extra chip, and you didn't call Mr. Eckman?"

A puzzled look casually surfaced on Sweeney's face. His eyebrows lifted. "Okay, you're thinking, what if old man Sweeney just sticks the extra chip into his pocket and goes home with it? Right?" He wiggled his index finger at them and trotted out the door.

The super sleuths glanced at each other and followed.

Mr. Sweeney turned and locked the door behind them. "Follow me." Several steps later he pointed to a door that led to the outside. A nearby wall supported a time clock. "See that door? That's where all employees enter in the morning and leave in the afternoon." He waited for that thought to settle in. "Now, see that metal archway five feet back from the door?" He paused. "That's a metal detector." He raised his chin and swallowed. "If the bell goes off when I or anyone else passes through it, you better have either coins or a set of keys in your pocket." His eyes crept over the teenagers and his mouth produced a sluggish grin.

Joyce kept writing.

"So no one can get out of the factory with stolen parts," said Brian.

The old man nodded.

"How about Mr. Eckman?" asked Sammy.

Sweeney generated a surprise expression and then frowned. "He's the boss. You think he's going to steal from himself?"

Joyce kept writing.

"Hey, how's it going?" came a voice from a doorway. Andy Good moved toward them. "I'm to take you up to the Research and Development if you're finished with Joseph."

"I think we have enough for now," said Joyce, scanning her notes.

The old man shook their hands and bid them a warm good-bye. He turned in the direction of the locked door and over his shoulder said, "Come back and see me . . . if I'm still here."

"Just keep breathing," said Brian to the old man's back. "That's the secret of living—keep breathing."

The old man's right hand started to rise. Half way up it quivered and fell back to his pocket. He found his key, unlocked his door, and disappeared inside.

Entering the Research and Development Department was eerie. The festive atmosphere seen at their last visit was missing. All the engineers were in their own little cubicles, working.

"Now that Smarty Pants is in his final testing phase, we have a cool-down period," said Andy Good as he invited the teens into his office. "It's an occasion to relax and enjoy the success of Smarty Pants. Of course, at the same time we try to come up with another ingenious toy idea."

Sammy noticed that Andy Good's office was the same as Dale Martin's office. The same desk, the same worktable, and the same shelves containing bits and pieces of electronic toys. "Are all the engineering offices the same here?" he asked.

"All the same. First we brainstorm as a group, and then we work independently. Sometimes we end up working in pairs, like Dale Martin and I did on Smarty Pants. In the end we all come together and pool our results."

"How long have you worked here?" asked Joyce, without looking up from her note-taking.

"About a year," said Andy, backing up and sitting on his desk. He combed his fingers through his dark curls. "Last time you were here you were looking for a bear." Andy paused. "And now you're back as reporters. Are the two connected?"

Without hesitating, Joyce replied. "No. The *Lancaster Sunday News* buys special interest articles that I write from time to time. It's true we were here inquiring about a bear, but then we got caught up in the excitement over Smarty Pants. We decided the toy factory would make a great feature for the *Sunday News*."

Andy made a sour face. "How old are you?" he asked.

"Fifteen," replied Joyce.

"You talked Mr. Eckman into letting you do this, but I personally don't like the idea."

"Let me guess," said Sammy. "You don't want the news about Smarty Pants to leak out."

"Once the news is out," said Andy, "any other company working on a similar idea will try to market their toy first. And that can put a big dent into any advertising campaign that's put together for Smarty Pants."

"You say other companies work on similar ideas," said Sammy. "Aren't they aware that you are too?"

"I suppose so."

"Then wouldn't they already be in a rush to market their toy?" asked Sammy.

"Probably, but . . . I still don't like the idea."

Sammy wondered if Mr. Good was concerned for the company or did he have personal reasons for not wanting the article written? "You don't have to worry. We promised Mr. Eckman we won't mention Smarty Pants in the article."

Andy took a deep breath. "I feel better already."

"May we see Mr. Martin now?" asked Sammy.

Andy glanced across the aisle to see if the head of the department was busy. He wasn't. "Follow me," said Andy, and he escorted the teens to his boss's office.

Dale looked up, leaned to his left, and made a set of plans vanish into the bottom desk drawer. He then stood, smiled, and shook hands with his expected company. "Greg Eckman said you'd be up to see me. And I was instructed to help you with an article you're writing." He pointed to the three chairs he had waiting for them. "Sit down. Sit down."

Joyce raised her camera. "Before I sit, may I take a picture of you and Mr. Good?"

Dale looked at the papers exposed on his desk. "Okay, Andy, come over here."

When Andy Good rested his hand on Dale's shoulder, Joyce moved to her left and snapped off three shots. "Thanks," she said as she sat and rested her camera on the floor.

Mr. Eckman stretched his head around Andy, who was now standing at the open doorway. "How are you kids doing?" he asked. "How's the story coming along?"

"Great," answered Joyce. "You have quite a factory here."

"Remember, in your story, no mention of Smarty Pants. I don't want the competition to learn of our newest creation."

"It will be a great story without Smarty Pants," said Sammy.

Dale Martin glanced at Joyce. "Did you name your dog yet?"

Joyce looked confused. "What? Oh, the toy dog. Yes, I gave him a name."

Sammy and Brian showed interest also.

"Mike. His name is Mike," she said. "Years ago we had a real dog named Mike, but he died."

"So his name lives on," said Dale. "What did you name the rabbit?"

Joyce displayed a grin as she looked to her left. "Well, Brian, what did you name your rabbit?"

"Hey, I gave the rabbit to my sister," said Brian quickly. "I don't know what she'll name it."

Joyce winked at the three men then confronted her friend. "You gave the rabbit to your sister? I thought you had it at home on your bed."

"Yeah, your mother said you can't go to sleep without it," said Sammy.

"Ha, ha," said Brian. He glanced up at the men, who were enjoying the personal joke. "I gave the rabbit to my ten-year-old sister this morning. She was mad because my mother was taking her to visit our aunt in Lancaster. My sister didn't want to go so I gave her the rabbit. I told her it would bring her good luck."

The mood changed quickly. Dale reached up and grabbed a monkey from the shelf. "Here's a monkey for you, Brian, for being so thoughtful."

While Brian hated to turn down the offer, he didn't want to be considered a sissy. He shook his head. "No, that's okay. Thanks anyway."

"On that note," said Greg Eckman, "I will leave you alone to continue the interview." He stared at Andy Good.

"Ah, yeah, I better get back to work." Andy turned and entered his office.

"I saw you put away some papers when we came in," said Sammy. "Is that your next toy idea?"

"We always have the next electronic concept waiting in the wings," said Dale. "But the question is, can we make it work? That's what we try to do here in Research and Development—make things work."

Joyce's pen was zipping over the yellow tablet. "How many people do you have in your department?" she asked.

"Ten. That includes me."

Joyce knew the kind of questions she must ask to get certain answers. "The last time we were here, I noticed the assortment of electronic parts and stuffed animals you have here in your office. How do you get them?"

Joyce's question raised Dale's eyebrows. "I expected your next question to be, How much money do you make?" said the engineer.

"How much do you make?" asked Brian.

"Not as much as you think," answered Dale.

Brian waited, thinking Mr. Martin would disclose his earnings, but Dale just looked at Brian.

"That's why I didn't ask that question," said Joyce. "I figured it was too personal."

Dale smiled, "The software and hardware for the toys are ordered ahead of time. We're told when they come in, and we write out a form. The list is then taken down to Joseph Sweeney, who fills out the order."

"So you take all these parts and somehow come up with a mechanized toy that sells."

"Some of the toys today are more like little computers," said Brian.

A sadness fell over the engineer. "Yes, my father thinks they are more like electronic gadgets than the toys of his day." Dale produced a small framed picture from the desk drawer. "This is my father. He used to own this business."

"Martin," said Brian. "Martin Toys."

Dale nodded, his eyes downcast. "My dad had medical problems. The bills piled up. He went deeper and deeper in debt. He finally sold the business to Greg Eckman." He sighed and slipped the picture back into the drawer. "Dad's in a nursing home now."

"So you continued working here for Mr. Eckman," said Sammy.

"Yes, I went to college, got my engineering degree, and returned to help Dad. I was in the process of updating our toy line when Dad got seriously ill. He needed money badly so he sold the company. The new owner, Mr. Eckman, liked my ideas so he kept me on. Some of the employees here worked for my father."

Joyce was writing frantically.

"You don't have to put that in the story," said Dale, watching the young girl struggle to record his every word.

"Are you kidding?" asked Brian. "This is great—"

Sammy figured where Brian was going with his train of thought so he quickly said, "We can decide later whether we want to use it." He looked at Dale. "Unless you'd rather we not include your father in the story."

"No, that will be okay. Dad will like that."

"Is there a restroom here I can use?" asked Brian, shifting from one foot to the other.

"Yeah, out the door, down the steps, first door on your left," said Dale.

Brian hurried downstairs and found the men's restroom. When he came out again into the hallway, he heard a faint voice. It was coming from the women's restroom next door. The words he heard were, "The kids are here."

Brian stiffened. He moved closer to the door.

" . . . upstairs. I never dealt with teenagers before." A short pause. "Yeah, I'll watch out." Another pause. "Yes, I know they're intelligent. What if they stumble onto the truth before they leave here today?"

The voice paused for a long time. Brian guessed the woman was talking to someone on a cell phone. He waited, straining his ear at the door. And then . . .

"Okay, if that's what you want, Danny Boy. I'll take care of them."

# CHAPTER ELEVEN

Brian shook. He swallowed hard and took a deep breath. He had no doubt the voice was referring to them. The words, "I'll take care of them," played again and again in his head.

His first instinct was to run up the steps and tell Sammy and Joyce what he had heard. But in his panic an idea formed. He would go back into the restroom and wait for the woman to leave. He would peek out the door, see her, and be able to identify her later. But when Brian reentered the men's room, he discovered the door opened the wrong way. He heard the woman leave, but by the time he stuck his head around the door, someone's back was disappearing into the Assembly Room.

He'd know that back anywhere, he thought. Short dark hair, a tan wrap-around skirt, and white sneakers.

Sammy and Joyce had finished with Mr. Martin and were descending the stairs with Andy

Good. He had been instructed to take the teenagers on a tour of the Assembly Room on the first floor.

When Sammy saw Brian's bewildered look, he asked, "Didn't you make it in time?"

"What? . . . Oh, yeah, . . . I . . . Hey, come here." Brian beckoned to Sammy and Joyce.

Andy Good waited while the teens had a little conference. He made no attempt to overhear them.

After Brian gave the details of his encounter with the ominous voice, the trio decided to take a quick tour of the Assembly Room and then leave. They would have to be extra careful. Sammy instructed Brian not to over-react if he saw the dark-haired woman, wearing a tan wrap-around and white sneakers.

The Assembly Room was exactly as the trio had seen it the previous day. Both men and women were seated at long worktables. Everything was clean. The precise movements of the workers indicated the delicate work that went into the assembly of the toys. One group was responsible for installing a mechanical device into each furry critter. Another group installed the circuit boards. After the computer chips containing the software were soldered and implanted into the furry animals, each assembled creature was tested.

Sammy shook his head as he scoured the many workstations in the room. So many suspects to be considered. True, these employees had no direct connection to the receiving of the smuggled chips, but they couldn't be discounted. The pile of parts at each workstation told him that everyone was a suspect.

Impatiently, Brian pointed to work table number four. "There she is," he whispered as he flapped his elbow into Sammy. "Short dark hair, white sneakers, and she's wearing a tan dress."

"Brian, haven't you noticed? They're all wearing tan smocks, men and women," said Sammy. He waved his hand. "And look at all the white sneakers."

Joyce stopped taking notes long enough to look up and to add her own observations. "It must be part of their work uniforms. Look at that woman at number sixteen," she said. "Her hair is short and she's wearing white shoes. Even there at number nineteen, she fits the description. There at—"

"Number sixteen," interrupted Brian. "There's something about her hair."

Joyce looked over at Andy Good, who was grinning. "Is it okay if we talk to some of the workers?"

Andy shrugged. "If they don't mind, it's okay with me."

"Number sixteen," said Joyce, smiling as she approached the woman. "Do you mind being a number?"

The middle-aged woman looked up and smiled. "No, I don't mind, but I wish it was my age. Hi, I'm Kim Rider."

The three teens introduced themselves and told of Joyce's mission as news reporter. Then Joyce asked, "Is it okay if I ask you some questions?"

Sammy saw Kim Rider hesitate, her facial muscles tightening slightly. "No, I don't mind, but I only started here last Wednesday. It might be better if you talked to a seasoned employee."

"You can give us the fresh viewpoint of a newcomer," said Joyce. "How do you like your job so far?" she asked quickly.

Kim Rider seemed to ignore the question. She pressed two wires against the battery terminal. A baby kangaroo popped its head out of its mother's pouch and said, "Hello, I'm ready to play." Kim tossed the tested toy into a nearby container on wheels, and without looking up, she shrugged. "It's okay. A job's a job I guess." She grabbed another kangaroo and prepared to turn another inert stuffed creature into a working electronic marvel.

"Do you drive to work?" asked Joyce.

Kim hesitated. "I have a friend who drops me off." She slipped the electronic components through the slit of the furry cloth.

"May I ask you where you live?" asked Joyce.

Kim's hands paused. Her eyes slid from the animal to Joyce. "Is this story you're writing about me or about Eckman's Electronic Toy Factory?" She added a smile to take the edge off the sarcasm.

"Without employees there'd be no factory," said Joyce. "I thought the public might like knowing how far some of the employees travel to work."

"Just say I live in Lancaster, about five miles away."

Brian couldn't contain himself any longer. "Do you live with Danny Boy?" he asked.

Sammy and Joyce cringed at first when Brian blabbed it out. If this was the person Brian had overheard, they didn't want her to know they were on to her. But, it was the only option open to them. How else to discover if this was the right person?

Kim Rider flinched for a second, recovered, and then replied, "My husband's name is George, and I have no child named Danny."

Sammy knew she was lying.

"Oops," said Brian. "I thought you were someone else. Sorry."

Joyce continued the interview, asking questions about the factory and not about Kim's personal life. Mrs. Rider confirmed the fact that when supplies were needed at her station, she filled out a form, gave it to a foreman, and the materials were brought to her workstation. Joyce finished the interview by snapping two pictures of Kim Rider.

The teens then followed the man who pushed the filled containers of toys to the Packing Department. It was not a special room but rather the area at the end of the assembly line. They watched as individual toys were placed into boxes and the boxes placed into cartons. The cartons were then stacked against the side wall.

Another group of workers applied addressed shipping labels to the cartons and sent them on their way to Marty Shipman in Shipping and

Receiving. That brought the trio back to where they started.

"Teamwork," said Brian. "That's what makes it a success—teamwork."

"That's great, Brian. I'll emphasize that in my article," said Joyce, adding to her notes.

Sammy glanced back at workstation sixteen. "That same teamwork could work against us. Let's not forget that somewhere in the team lurks a rotten apple."

When Brian and Joyce looked back to see what had caused Sammy to make that statement, Brian added, " . . . a rotten apple or *two*."

At workstation sixteen Andy Good and Kim Rider were deep in conversation.

# CHAPTER TWELVE

The Bird-in-Hand Farmers Market was a mixture of sights and smells. Locals blended with tourists, angling for space at the stands. Brenda's Snack Counter was no exception. All the counter stools were occupied. The three young detectives sat at the end, just inside the door.

Brenda's face peered over the three hot dogs with sauerkraut on the side. She was a small, slender woman in her forties with short blond hair. "Now that you're famous detectives, I don't see much of you. Don't you have time for us common people anymore?" Brenda playfully displayed a frown and a protruding lower lip as she placed the paper plates on the counter.

"Yeah, this might be the last time we come in here, Brenda," kidded Brian. "From now on we'll be eating our hot dogs at the country club."

Brenda winked at Joyce then leaned toward Sammy and Brian. "Word's going around that you boys need the help of a girl to help you solve your cases."

Brian almost fell off the stool. "Hey, it's teamwork," he said. "We work as a team. Right, Sammy?"

Sammy nodded. "Brenda, what do you know about the Eckman Electronic Toy Factory?"

"Are you working a case there?" she asked.

Sammy didn't want to lie so he said, "Joyce is writing an article about the factory for the newspaper. We just came from there."

"I only know what I read in the newspaper," said Brenda. "Old man Martin got sick, needed money, and sold the business to this Eckman fellow. I heard Eckman is immature, but it's just an act. He can be pretty ruthless."

The trio nodded in agreement and started to eat.

Brenda collected the money from the counter. "Good luck with your investigation," she said as she turned away and returned to the lunch trade. Her sly grin indicated that she knew the three teens were working a case involving the toy factory. That's one secret she would keep to herself.

After the super sleuths ate their lunch, they agreed to meet at Moore Bears at five o'clock for their meeting with Agent Ted Manners.

Sammy helped his parents in the shop for the rest of the afternoon. Joyce developed and printed the pictures she had taken at the factory.

Brian took a nap and dreamed that he, Helm, Brian Helm, agent double-oh-seven and a half, had solved the case. Through ingenious deduction, downright hard work, and a note from his mother, secret agent Helm found CRACKERJACK, the classified computer module. He arrested Joseph Sweeney. CRACKERJACK was in the shape of a key on Sweeney's key ring.

At five-twenty, John Moore locked the front door of the shop. He hurried back to his office, closed the door, and joined the other four at the table. Agent Manners sat at the head of the table, facing Joyce and Brian to his right and Sammy and John to his left.

"You'll notice the absence of Julie Greenleaf," said Manners, all business-like. "She returned to Philly. Her work is done here." The agent unzipped his briefcase and slid out a light-green tablet and a pen. "Okay, what do you have to report? Any luck?"

"First of all," said Sammy, "Mr. Eckman liked the idea of us doing a story about him and the factory. We had to promise not to write about Smarty Pants. He doesn't want a rival company to learn he's getting ready to market a new toy sensation. He arranged for us to visit the different departments and interview some of the employees."

"Sounds like you had an interesting morning. Did you come up with any clues?"

"Yeah," said Brian. "I heard a lady talking to a Danny—"

Sammy touched Brian's arm. "It might be better if we start with what we found out in the Shipping and Receiving Department," interrupted Sammy. "The order in which things happened might be important."

"Very true," said Manners, taking notes.

Sammy nodded to Joyce. "Joyce, you have your notes. Suppose you do the talking." Sammy had two reasons for appointing Joyce the spokesperson. One, to make her feel part of the team. Two, he wanted to hear the information repeated by another person. A fresh telling of the facts might reveal a missed clue.

The young female detective checked for the agent's attention. She had it. "Marty Shipman is a one-man Shipping and Receiving Department. He would be in the ideal position to pocket the intelligence chip. He checks in the shipments arriving at the factory and checks all the boxes leaving the building."

"But he doesn't open—" said Brian before Sammy interrupted him.

"What Brian means to say," said Sammy, "is that Marty Shipman *said* he doesn't open the boxes. But, in fact, he could if he wanted to. It would be easy for him to reseal them before he sent them on to Inventory."

The FBI agent nodded and added to his notes.

Joyce picked up one of two large envelopes from the table and handed it to Manners. She slid the other across to Sammy and John. "These are the pictures I took today. The top five are of Marty Shipman."

"You say his name is Shipman," said Ted Manners, taking great interest in the photos.

"Yeah, it really is," said Brian without any further comment.

The agent pulled a folder from his case and opened it. "We ran the list of employees' names through our criminal records, names that Julie Greenleaf pulled from the factory computer." He scanned through the papers. "Marty Shipman, now twenty-eight, was arrested for stealing a car when he was seventeen. No arrests since then."

Joyce continued. "The next three photos show Joseph Sweeney in Inventory. He keeps a running count of all goods received and dispersed throughout the factory. Every box is opened and counted. Mr. Sweeney is another possible suspect."

"You're a good photographer," said John Moore, examining the photos.

The agent shook his head at a photo. His finger followed the shelving that lined the walls. "Our task seems impossible when you think that the smuggled chip could be in any one of these bins."

"The chip isn't doing anyone any good if it's in one of those bins," said Sammy.

"My thoughts exactly," said Manners. "That's why we believe the chip was sent to the toy factory because shipments from there go around the world. It's a natural for smuggling stolen computer parts to anywhere on the globe. To China, for example."

"But you searched the shipment to China and the intelligence chip wasn't there," said Brian.

"No, it wasn't. Something happened. For some reason the chip wasn't included in the order."

"If that's true," said Joyce, "then CRACKER-JACK is still there in the factory."

"If the module missed the shipment to China," said Brian, "why not just stick it in an envelope addressed China and mail it at the post office?"

Manners leaned back in his chair and clasped his hands behind his head. "First of all, you don't stick a billion-dollar intelligence module into an envelope. You have to pack it carefully so there's no damage to the chip. No one is going to walk out of the factory with a small box in his hand. Even in an envelope, you couldn't get it out of the factory. Did they show you the metal detector they use to ensure no one leaves the building with parts of any kind?"

"What about the custodians?" asked Sammy. "When they leave at night, who checks them out?"

"No one," said the agent. "They are bonded. If they skip out with any merchandise, the insurance company reimburses the company."

Brian sat tall in his chair and gave a cough or two as he remembered his dream. "I know who and how someone could have walked out with the chip in his pocket."

Brian now had everyone's attention. "Who and how?" asked Sammy.

The grin on Brian's face widened. He stood to dramatize his explanation. "Mr. Sweeney opens the box that contains the chip." Brian went through the motions of opening a box. "Ah, he finds the marked module." A look of satisfaction rippled across Brian's face. "He takes a set of keys from his pocket," said Brian as he searched his own pocket for something to substitute for keys. He pulled out a pen. "Mr. Sweeney fastens the module to the head of one key." Brian spit on the tip of his thumb and pressed it against the pen.

Ted Manners stood and added some dramatics of his own by continuing Brian's story. "So when it's time to go home, Sweeney goes up to the metal detector, hands his keys and coins to the inspector, walks through the detector where his coins and keys are returned to him. He then walked home with CRACKERJACK attached to the keys."

"Yeah, pretty good, huh?" said Brian.

"Yeah, pretty good," repeated Manners, " . . . except for one thing. CRACKERJACK is two inches square and a quarter inch thick. And that's by itself. So the module isn't damaged, it's packaged in a static shield bag. Even a flow of static electricity could ruin the chips."

Joyce quickly changed the subject. "After Inventory, we went to Research and Development." She indicated the next photos. "We talked to Andy Good and Dale Martin. Dale Martin is the head of that division. They and the other eight engineers work with all kinds of parts."

"Dale Martin's father was the previous owner of the toy factory," said Sammy. He repeated what Mr. Martin had told them about his father.

The agent added the information to his notes then looked at Brian. "What were you saying earlier about Danny Boy?"

"I heard a voice coming from the women's restroom. A woman was talking on a cell phone to someone called Danny Boy. She talked about us being there at the factory. I only got to see the back of her as she rushed into the Assembly Room."

Joyce waited for Manners to react. When he frowned but said nothing, she said, "That's where we went next. They have about forty workstations where they assemble the toys. Brian thought the woman he had seen was at station number sixteen." Joyce checked her notes then pointed to the picture in front of the agent. "Her name is Kim Rider."

"Kim Rider," repeated Manners as he inspected the picture. He checked his folder. "She has no police record." He looked again at Brian. "She could have been in contact with someone in the building or outside. Do you have any idea who this Danny Boy is?"

John Moore spoke up for the first time. "Are there any Dans on your list of employees?"

Manners shuffled through his papers then selected one. "Hm, yeah. Name's Daniel Reed."

"What department does he work in?" asked Joyce.

"Research and Development. He has no criminal record," answered Manners.

"Looks like he's your only decent lead," said John.

Manners nodded as he flipped through the last remaining photos showing the Packing Department and several outside shots of the toy factory. "Without any proof we can't touch that building or the people inside. We had our one chance at Greg Eckman's computer and a chance using you three. Customs can continue to inspect any more shipments going to China. That's our only real hope for CRACKERJACK to be recovered." Ted Manners gathered up the pictures, placed them back into the manila envelope, and stuck it inside his briefcase.

"What's happening at Argus Solutions, where CRACKERJACK was produced?" asked Sammy.

The agent stood. "Our informant is someone we have placed inside Argus Solutions. All he knows is that Argus management reported a top secret module missing. Our informant traced it to a possible order of chips going to the Eckman Electronic Toy Factory. And that's what we followed up on. Because it involved national security, we got a court order to investigate the toy factory."

"Wasn't your informant at Argus able to track down the person who stole the chip?" asked Sammy.

Manners shook his head. "Argus Solutions is conducting their own investigation, and so far they have come up with nothing. If we can catch the person here, it could lead us back to the person they're looking for."

Sammy never felt more at a loss than he felt at that moment. He had no key puzzle pieces to add to the puzzle. True, he had learned how a toy factory operated. He had met some interesting people and a toy named Smarty Pants. But where were the clues? Had he missed something? Sammy was not ready to face a dead end to the case. He was not about to give up. In fact, the young detective was at his best under pressure.

The faraway look in Sammy's blue eyes made Brian and Joyce suspect he was constructing another plan.

"Well, what's our next step?" asked Brian. "You have a plan. Right, Sammy?"

"I was just thinking," said Sammy. "We have an appointment with Mr. Eckman for our story interview tomorrow morning. That might be our last chance to question him."

"And?" said Brian, knowing Sammy had something up his sleeve.

"Mr. Eckman doesn't go through the metal detector. He can just walk out of the building with the chip in his pocket. He can box it and mail it to China." Sammy raised his hand. "But, if he did, there's a chance customs would inspect it and trace the box back to him."

"Not if the return address was of a vacant lot," said Joyce.

"We already covered that possibility," said Manners proudly. "We watched Eckman. He made no trips to the post office or a mailbox."

Sammy pulled a picture from his pile. "Look here." He pointed to neatly stacked packages on the floor beside Marty Shipman. "Those packages are waiting for the mail truck to arrive." Sammy looked at Ted Manners. "Was all the mail inspected or just that one shipment to China?"

The agent's face hardened. "With national security involved, *all* packages leaving the factory were inspected," he said.

Sammy's hopes were shattered. Reluctantly he stood and headed for the door. His two friends followed.

"We'll meet again here tomorrow after five," said Manners. "Maybe you'll have something by then."

*Yeah, a sign that says dead end*, thought Brian.

The super sleuths didn't know it, but that sign would soon announce a newly constructed highway.

# CHAPTER THIRTEEN

When the three teenage detectives entered the reception area, Molly Day was neat, trim, and all smiles. This came as a shock to the trio. The last time they had seen the middle-aged receptionist her hair was a mess, her dress was long and drab, and she wore no makeup.

But that morning Molly Day actually looked human. Her dress was short and colorful. Her hair was styled to complement her face with its hint of makeup.

"Well, good morning," said Molly. "Take a seat and I'll tell Mr. Eckman that you're here." She quickly disappeared into the office.

Sammy, the detective, wondered if Molly was being overly nice because she was hiding something. Joyce, the photographer-reporter, wondered if Molly was trying to get her picture taken for the news story. Brian, secret agent, wondered if Molly was after his autograph.

As they all sat waiting with their private thoughts, Joyce gave Brain one last warning. "And remember, don't go near that stuffed dog on Mr. Eckman's desk."

Before Brian could reply, Molly came bounding out of the office, closing the door behind her. "Mr. Eckman will see you in a couple of minutes." She glanced at the camera hanging from Joyce's shoulder. "It's okay to take pictures now," she said as she ran her hand back over her hair and then smoothed out the wrinkles in her dress.

When no reply came from the teenagers, she added, "Oh, I don't mean now, but for the story you're writing. Mr. Eckman said you're allowed to photograph what you need for the article." Molly returned to her desk. She rearranged her nameplate, sat up straight, and forced an uncomfortable smile.

And no one had told her to say cheese, thought Joyce.

A woman entered the room. She went straight to Molly. "I'm here to see Greg," she announced.

"Oh, yes," said Molly. "Go right in."

The woman ushered herself into Mr. Eckman's private office.

Sammy leaned over and whispered. "Did you see who that was?"

"Yeah, Linda Baker," said Brian.

"Do they sell electronic toys in their Amish Country Crafts store?" asked Joyce.

"I don't think so," said Sammy, shaking his head.

"Hey, we were supposed to be next to see Mr. Eckman," said Brian, staring at Molly.

Molly Day shrugged then smiled.

Sammy recognized an important puzzle piece when he saw one. And boy, was this one—a definite straightedge piece. He snapped some previous pieces together. An intelligence chip module was stolen, code name: CRACKERJACK. It was smuggled into the Eckman Electronic Toy Factory for shipment to China. Linda Baker had Joyce take a passport picture. Mrs. Baker was going overseas. She's now in "Greg" Eckman's office. Was her destination China? wondered the super sleuth.

The young detective brushed his hair back and whispered, "I'm going to the restroom." He stood and headed for the hallway. "Okay if I use your restroom?" he asked as he passed Molly.

"Sure," she said, waving her hand. "Down the hall, third door on your right."

When Sammy was around the corner and hidden from Molly's view, he stopped at the first door. This was the side door to Mr. Eckman's office. He knelt and untied his shoe. He put his ear to the door and listened.

" . . . and the man you want to see is Woo Chung. He knows you're coming and will be at the airport to meet you. Don't forget to bow. And please guard it carefully."

Sammy had heard enough, and he certainly didn't want to get caught listening at the door. He tied his shoe and walked to the men's restroom. At the door he turned around and walked back to the reception area. He was ready to reclaim his seat when Linda Baker rushed from the office.

They were face to face.

"Hi, Mrs. Baker," said Sammy.

"Hi," repeated Brian and Joyce from their chairs.

Linda's face got red. Her breath was short. She swallowed hard. The box she held with both hands wavered back and forth like it was a hot potato.

"Oh, careful," said Sammy as he sprang forward and steadied the box.

Greg Eckman stuck his head out the door. "I'll see the *Sunday News* reporters now," he said with a childish voice. Then in a stern voice he strained, "Good-bye, Linda."

The office was still a mess, but Mr. Eckman wore his coat and tie. His hair was freshly combed, as was his mustache. "You probably want a picture of me here at the desk," he said, holding Honey, the breakaway dog. He held the dog to his face. "Yes, you, too, are going to have your picture taken, sweet thing."

The first shot of him kissing the dog was strictly for Joyce's scrapbook. The tall, bulky man holding a little cuddly dog made the second shot look like an advertisement for tissues—TOUGH

BUT SOFT. Shot three had Honey balanced on Mr. Eckman's head.

Joyce lowered her camera. She could see the headline now: TOYS THAT TURN ADULTS INTO CHILDREN.

Sammy didn't want to mention Mrs. Baker's visit and what he had heard at the door. If he did, the chip module might go into hiding again. Instead, he asked, "What made you buy out Martin Toys?"

With Sammy's question, Greg Eckman released Honey back on the desk. He smoothed his mustache with several fingers and reverted to a business-like attitude. "To make money," he answered. "With the world becoming computerized, I saw the future of electronic toys."

"I have a problem with that," said Joyce as she stopped writing. "I liked my toys better when I controlled what they said and did. They were an extension of me. They helped me express myself. They could say, do, and go, according to my imagination. I feel today's electronic toys control me."

"And Smarty Pants?" asked Mr. Eckman. "You don't think he's a great toy?"

"That's my point," said Joyce. "Smarty Pants isn't really a toy. A toy is something a child can play with. Children won't be allowed to touch Smarty Pants. It might disturb the electronic components inside. They can't play with it in the back yard. They can't get it dirty. They can't take it to bed with them." Joyce paused before she said, "Yes,

Smarty Pants is a great teaching machine—but it's not a toy."

"Are you suggesting I change the name of my company?" asked Eckman.

"It could be easier than changing the definition of what a toy is," said Joyce smiling.

Sammy thought that Joyce's honesty might offend Mr. Eckman until he saw the big smile developing. His raw laughter filled the office.

Brian was hoping it wasn't the laughter of a madman ready to do them in.

The laughter stopped as Eckman pointed his finger. "That could be the theme of your next news story: Smarty Pants, the toy that changed the definition of the word toy."

Joyce frowned, "I'll have to think about that, Mr. Eckman," she said as she started a new page of notes in her yellow tablet. "What did you do before you bought the factory?"

Leaning back in his chair, Greg Eckman looked embarrassed. "Nothing."

"Nothing?" repeated Joyce. Her words were joined by surprised looks from Sammy and Brian.

"I traveled a lot." Eckman paused. "I inherited a lot of money. My father was an investment broker. He made a fortune investing other people's money."

"So why now?" asked Joyce. "Why, at this point in your life, did you decide to go to work?"

Eckman lowered his head. "I got tired of traveling. I got tired of playing with my model trains. I got tired of being constantly around my wife and kids."

Were those tears glistening on Eckman's manly cheeks? Brian wondered. To console the man, Brian said, "Yeah, I know what you mean. I love my parents, but I don't want to hang out with them."

Brian's remark brought strange looks from his friends. He shrugged, raised his eyebrows, and then grinned.

"You should be very proud that your company has developed Smarty Pants," said Sammy.

Eckman leaned forward and raised his eyebrows. "Remember, you're not to mention Smarty Pants in this article. Months from now you can, when we're ready to introduce him to the world. If word got out before, our competition would . . ."

"We understand that, Mr. Eckman," said Joyce. "We won't—"

The phone on the desk rang. Eckman picked it up quickly and listened. His face reddened. "How could they?" he roared. "Yes, I will." He slammed down the receiver and stood. "That was my wife." The button he pushed on the remote turned on a small television set across the room. Channel 8 had a new conference in progress.

" . . . and now, Paul Bowman, head of Research and Development here at Thunder Boom Toys, will give you the details." A blond, thin man stood at the podium. He displayed a white toothy smile. The drawing he held up was of a toy dog dressed in clothes and sitting at a desk. "Smart Alex was developed by our Research Department. Smart Alex, the electronic dog, will print or write at the sound of your voice. Any five-year-old can talk to this electronic dog and Smart Alex will write or print what the child says."

"I can't believe it!" shouted Eckman, wiping his brow. "They stole our idea, and now they'll put it on the market before we get ours out."

"And when you do come out with Smarty Pants, Thunder Boom Toys will say you stole from them," said Sammy.

"You bet they will," said Eckman as he rushed to the door and flung it open. "Molly, I want all the Research and Development people in the conference room in ten minutes. Call my lawyer and tell him to get here as quickly as possible." He looked back at the trio. "We'll have to postpone our interview until another time."

"Sure, we understand," said Sammy. "But could I ask, up to this point, who could have gotten their hands on the complete set of blueprints of Smarty Pants?"

Eckman's eyes looked up and to the right. "Only myself and a handful of engineers had access to the plans," he answered. "If you three can find out how Thunder Boom Toys got them and can prove it, we'll beat them at their own game."

"Is your computer used for the development of your electronic toys?" asked Sammy.

"Of course," said Eckman. "The whole Smarty Pants program is on computer."

"Do you use a network of computers?" asked Joyce.

"Look, I don't have time to go into this now," said Eckman. "I have a major catastrophe on my hands here." He motioned Molly. "My friends are leaving. Make an appointment for two days from now." He glanced at the trio. They nodded. "I'll be in the conference room upstairs." He rushed down the hall and scrambled up the steps, two at a time.

"What's all the excitement about?" asked Molly as the teens approached her desk.

"Another company is coming out with a toy similar to one you're developing," said Sammy.

Molly shrugged, checked the calendar, and filled out an appointment card for their next visit.

"Who operates the computer in the office?" asked Sammy.

"Why, Greg . . . ah, Mr. Eckman."

"Are the computers upstairs hooked into this one?"

"Yeah, the guys up in R and D use . . ." Molly's eyes grew cold. "I don't think I should talk to you about that."

"I'm sorry, Molly. May I call you Molly?" asked Sammy.

She nodded and smiled. "Everybody here at work does."

"I can see you're a very important person here at the toy factory," said Sammy. "Joyce, you should take some pictures of Molly for our article."

"Definitely," said Joyce, and she made a grand gesture of photographing the receptionist from various angles.

"I'll bet you're pretty good yourself with a computer," said Brian as he snatched up the yellow tablet.

Molly smiled as she watched the pen travel across the tablet. "Why, yes. Sometimes, Greg will have me enter receiving and inventory figures. I'm quite good at figures you know."

*It's too bad you don't have one*, thought Brian as he scribbled across the page.

Joyce hurriedly put the camera strap around her neck and took the tablet and pen from Brian. "I better take over. It's hard to read your writing."

"My full name is Molly Anne Day," said the receptionist, looking at Joyce.

Joyce wrote the full name and looked up. "I guess you see a lot of people going in and out of Mr. Eckman's office."

"That's part of my job."

"Down the hall there is a side door to the office. Is that used by employees?" asked Sammy.

"Yeah." Molly then pointed to the building's front entrance. "But anyone who comes in *that* door must go through me to see Mr. Eckman."

While the receptionist was busy talking to Brian and Joyce, Sammy toyed with the sign-in clipboard. He flipped through several pages before his blue eyes settled on a date three weeks earlier. And there it was.

Woo Chung, Hong Kong, China.

# *Chapter Fourteen*

Woo Chung of Hong Kong, China, was now the topic of discussion in Bird-in-Hand, Pennsylvania. The brain-storming session that afternoon began on the trio's bike ride back to Sammy's house.

Sammy reported to Brian and Joyce what he had heard at the office door. He told of the Chinese visitor from Hong Kong. They were excited, discussing how CRACKERJACK was probably hidden in a toy that Mrs. Baker was taking to Hong Kong. Sammy had tried to contact Ted Manners, but the agent was "unavailable." Since Linda Baker wasn't leaving on her trip for three days, they decided to wait for their five o'clock meeting to report their findings. Agent Manners could then confront Linda Baker, find the stolen module, and make the arrest.

Brian was still bouncing on the bed when he said, "And Mr. Eckman wanted us to believe he inherited his money from his father. Ha! The toy factory is a cover for his smuggling racket. That's how he gets his money."

"I can't believe Linda Baker would be part of something like this," offered Joyce, pushing her rocker into high gear.

"I always thought she had shifty eyes," said Brian.

Sammy leaned forward, elbows on his desk. "Did you notice? She's on a first-name basis with Mr. Eckman. She told Molly she wanted to see 'Greg.'"

"I bet they're partners in this smuggling business," said Brian.

Pushing aside the case of the stolen intelligence module, Sammy ventured into a new area: industrial espionage. A company stealing secrets from their competitors was nothing new. Lawsuits claiming corporations stole from other corporations have been filed for decades. Many claims were hard to prove. Sammy's dilemma was how his detective team could prove Smart Alex was a rip-off of Smarty Pants.

"Okay," he said, "the item for discussion now is, how did Thunder Boom Toys get their hands on the plans for Smarty Pants?"

Brian clicked his heels together. "Hey, maybe Mr. Eckman stole the idea from Thunder Boom Toys."

"I don't think so," said Sammy.

"What makes you say that?" asked Brian.

"Thunder Boom didn't have a working model. They only showed a picture of the dog."

"It's possible that Thunder Boom Toys has an engineer at Eckman's toy factory reporting back to them," said Joyce.

"Detective Phillips can check their bank accounts," said Brian. "See if any large deposits of money have been made recently. Right, Sammy?"

"Sounds like a good idea," said Sammy, making a note to visit their friend, Detective Ben Phillips.

Now that the brainstorming was getting into new territory, Brian relaxed back on the bed. He focused on the ceiling and said, "I think it was Dale Martin."

"Why?" asked Joyce.

"Well, think about it. He's mad at Mr. Eckman for buying his father's business. The business that someday would have been his."

"You have a point there, Brian," said Joyce. "Maybe he's trying to bankrupt the business so he can buy it back at a bargain."

Brian sat up on the bed. "Sure, he sells the plans to Thunder Boom Toys for a half million, waits for Eckman Electronic Toy Factory to go under, then buys it back."

Sammy had another thought. "I don't think Mr. Martin is the revengeful type. Let's say Smarty Pants is worth five hundred thousand dollars to Thunder Boom Toys. That's enough motivation for anyone to betray the company they work for. The way I see it, anyone who had access to the Smarty Pants project is a suspect."

The rocker came to a stop. Joyce turned a new page in her note pad and wrote a name. "Let's make a list. I have Molly Day first."

"Dale Martin," said Brian, adding, "Andy Good."

"Don't forget Mr. Eckman," said Sammy as Joyce hurriedly wrote the names.

Brian rattled off a list of people. "Mr. Shipman, Mr. Sweeney, and supervisors from the assembly room."

"Brian," said Joyce, "don't get carried away."

Brian's head snapped up from the bed. "Hey, remember the side door to Mr. Eckman's office? Any of those guys could walk in. And let's say Mr. Eckman isn't there. They see the computer and get ideas."

"You're forgetting something, Brian," said Joyce. "They have to know the password to enter the programs in the computer."

Brian's head relaxed back on the bed as he again scanned the ceiling. "Well, maybe the password . . . okay, you're right," finally giving up.

"I don't know if they call them blueprints anymore," said Sammy, "but Mr. Martin kept a copy of the plans in his desk drawer."

Brian's head lifted again, and he looked at Joyce. "Yeah, and you don't need a password to get into that."

"So I'll add the engineers in R and D," said Joyce.

Sammy glanced down at his notes. "As we mentioned before, we'll have Detective Phillips check out some bank accounts. If we're lucky, someone on your list there, Joyce, might have some explaining to do."

"Yeah," added Brian, "how would you explain a bank balance of hundreds of thousands of dollars?"

Moore Bears closed at five o'clock. By five-fifteen the shop was empty except for John Moore and Ted Manners. Brian was late. Sammy and Joyce waited on the porch for their friend to arrive. Their spirits were high because of the good news they were about to report to Manners, and because Bigmoore, the big stuffed teddy bear, was back.

The FBI had done a decent restoration job. Bigmoore looked great. A long-lost friend had returned home. He didn't seem to mind at all being attached again to the porch wall by thin, wire cables.

It wasn't like Brian to be late. When he did finally arrive five minutes later, he was walking fast, was out of breath, and was carrying a rabbit. It was the same stuffed rabbit he had given his sister.

"Taking your rabbit out for a walk, Brian?" asked Joyce, displaying a mischievous grin.

Sammy knew that something was wrong. "What happened?" he asked.

Brian stepped up onto the porch and used his shirtsleeve to wipe the sweat from his face. "Some boy stole my bike." He pointed up the street. "I parked it outside the Bird-in-Hand Family Restaurant and went in to get a donut. When I came out, a boy was backing my bike across the parking lot. I ran and grabbed the handlebars to stop him, and he kicked me away. He crossed the road and disappeared behind the farm. I looked but I couldn't find him or my bike."

"Gee, Brian," said Joyce, "that's like someone stealing a police car from a policeman."

"Maybe they stole your bike, too," said Brian. "Where do you have it parked? At Sammy's house?"

Joyce stepped away from the porch and looked down the street. "Yep, and it's still there."

Sammy found it hard to believe that a boy from the area would steal Brian's bike. "Must be a tourist. Maybe he wants to travel the back roads to see the Amish."

Joyce was still in a teasing mood. "Or he wanted a souvenir from Brian Helm, local celebrity, and hot-shot detective, who carries around a stuffed rabbit."

"What are you doing with the rabbit?" asked Sammy. "I thought you gave it to your sister."

"She threw it at me today when she got home from visiting our aunt," said Brian. "She said the rabbit was bad luck."

"Why?" asked Joyce.

"My mother and sister helped my aunt pick cherries. My sister was on the ladder with the rabbit, and she fell off and broke her arm."

"And now your bike is stolen," said Joyce. "That rabbit *is* bad luck."

"I'd get rid of that thing if I were you," said Sammy.

"Hey, if Penn State can have Nittany, a lion, for a mascot, we can have Rubby, the rabbit, for ours."

"Rubby?" repeated Joyce.

"Sure, you rub him for good luck."

"But, your sister . . ."

"She rubbed him the wrong way," said Brian, demonstrating. "My sister rubbed him from front to back. That's bad luck. But, for good luck, you rub him from left to right."

"Okay, Brian," said Sammy, rolling his eyes, "from now on Rubby is our official mascot."

Joyce looked at the rabbit and then back at Brian. "You really don't believe in this luck thing, do you?"

Before Brian could answer, John Moore opened the door and stuck his head out. "You coming in? We're waiting for you."

The trio hustled in and joined the others in the office. Brian hid the rabbit under his chair. He didn't need any more rabbit humor.

Ted Manners, dressed in his gray business suit, showed some excitement in his voice as he said, "You tried to get me on the phone today. What's up?"

As Sammy's story unfolded, the agent cringed. "I should have made myself available for your call earlier. However, Linda won't be leaving for Hong Kong for several days."

"The man, who is to meet her in Hong Kong," said Sammy, "has the same name that I saw written on the visitor's clipboard at the reception desk. According to the sign-in sheet, Woo Chung was at the toy factory three weeks ago."

Manners was writing rapidly, recording what the young detective was saying. "You said the box Linda Baker carried had no markings on it."

"Right," said Sammy. "It was just a plain box."

"How big was it?" he asked without glancing up.

"Large enough to hold a fifteen- or eighteen-inch toy like Smarty Pants," said Sammy. "I helped Mrs. Baker steady the box so that I could feel its weight. It was much heavier than a box containing just a computer chip module and packing material."

Manners grinned. "CRACKERJACK is hidden inside a toy like Smarty Pants. It's made to look as if it belongs there. If the inspectors opened the box, they would miss seeing this particular module among the others." He stood quickly and added, "With what you just told me, I can get a court order to inspect that box."

Brian stood also and extended himself an extra two inches. He took a deep breath and tugged at his pants. "If you ever need help again, give us a call."

"We're glad we could be of help," said Sammy as he and Joyce rose to their feet. Then Sammy added, "If you find CRACKERJACK, I guess Kim Rider will be quitting her job."

"Yes, she . . ." Agent Manners stopped. "How did you know?"

"I wasn't positive until right now," said Sammy. "When we interviewed Kim Rider, she mentioned she was new to the job. She was only there a couple of days, which fit in with the FBI's involvement with the case. The last time we met, Brian was about to tell you of the conversation he overheard through the restroom door. I stopped him before he completed the code name said by the woman. Brian only got out the name Danny before I cut him off. Yet later, you used the name Danny Boy to refer back to the cell phone conversation."

"You mean he's Danny Boy, and Kim Rider is FBI?" asked Brian.

Sammy continued to stare at the agent, waiting for confirmation.

Ted Manners folded his arms across his chest. My code name is Danny Boy. Kim Rider, on assignment from FBI out of Chicago, is our inside plant at the toy factory."

"Has she turned up any leads?" asked Joyce.

"Not a one. She did talk to a lot of the employees—with no results. Recently, her job was to keep her eyes on you three, to protect you from any danger."

"It's strange," said Sammy. "At first, we thought she was the danger."

Agent Manners laughed and shook their hands. "Detective Ben Philips was right. You are smart, skillful, and highly motivated. You're the kind of people we need in the FBI."

Brian stood tall and smiled.

Manners added, "Come see me in five years."

Brian's height shrank and his smile wilted.

"See you, John," said the agent and vanished out the door.

"Boy, when they get what they want, they disappear," said Brian to whomever would listen.

Sammy shrugged. "And I wanted to mention another problem they're having at the factory."

"Oh, Ted's not really that bad," said John. "This is a high profile case. He's under a lot of pressure to show results. He needs to find CRACKERJACK and bring the case to a close."

"I can understand that," said Sammy.

John glanced down at the floor and with a twinkle in his eye said, "Oh, my, we have a traitor among us. Who would dare bring a bunny rabbit into a teddy bear shop?"

Rubby, the rabbit, was picked up quickly by Brian. "He's our mascot. Right, Sammy?" said Brian sheepishly.

"As long as he brings us good luck," said Sammy. "As long as he brings us good luck."

From the parked car across the street, the figure watched as the man in the gray suit left the bear shop. *Who was he?* wondered The Watcher. What connection did the man have with the meddling teenagers playing detective? The figure slipped lower in his seat as Sammy, Brian, and Joyce appeared on the porch. The Watcher raised a map to shield his face, the motion of a tourist.

It was because of the three super sleuths that CRACKERJACK was never included in the shipment to China. They had caused The Watcher great anxiety. Their identity had been no secret. Their past record of solving crimes was the talk of Bird-in-Hand. The Watcher didn't take them lightly.

A chuckle escaped the car as Brian threw the rabbit into the air and then caught it. The Watcher needed a laugh to release the stress. *Big crime fighters, still playing with toys,* thought The Watcher. *Good. Keep playing with your rabbit, and we'll see what happens tomorrow.*

After the trio headed for Sammy's house, The Watcher got out of the car, opened the trunk, and released Brian's bike to the sidewalk. The car pulled away from the curb and quickly disappeared down Main Street.

# CHAPTER FIFTEEN

It was getting dark, but the eight-year-old boy recognized the bike right away. Jonathan Chen was a big fan of Sammy and Brian and the bike was definitely Brian's. It was the only bike for miles that had a camouflage paint design.

Jonathan walked the bike across the street and down to Sammy's house. He leaned the bike against the old building and went away smiling. He had done his good deed for the day.

The next morning when Brian arrived at the house, he couldn't believe his good luck. His bike was back. It was scarred with scratches but that didn't matter. His old friend had returned.

On the ride to the police station with Sammy and Joyce, Rubby, the rabbit, rode the handlebars. Brian rambled on about how the rabbit was going to bring him good luck. Why, he could even fill the rabbit with secret stuff in case he was attacked or captured. "Hey," he yelled to the others. "You know what I could do with Rubby? I . . ."

Sammy and Joyce let out a sigh of relief when the police station came into view.

Thank goodness Rubby didn't take up much space. Brian was stuck again without a place to sit. Detective Phillips' office was only large enough for two extra chairs. Sammy and Joyce had already claimed those seats of honor. Brian had no choice but to hold the rabbit as he stood beside the desk.

Detective Phillips leaned to the side, making his chair screech with pain. He eyed the stuffed toy. "Hey, I see you caught 'Benny the Bunny,' the notorious bank bandit from Boston."

Brian was about to go into his spiel about Phanatic, the Philadelphia Phillies' mascot, and the Nittany Lion when he simply said, "No, he isn't 'Benny the Bunny.' He's 'Rubby the Rabbit.'" Brian set the twelve-inch furry animal on the desk.

"We already have a crime-fighting dog," said Phillips. "We don't need a crime-fighting rabbit."

"But you don't understand," said Joyce, winking at Detective Phillips. "Rubby is a good-luck rabbit. Brian had the good fortune of having his bike stolen and then returned."

Phillips grinned and took a sip of coffee. He twitched his thin mustache, raised his eyebrows, and aimed his penetrating eyes at Sammy. "I heard you all did another super job. I got a call from Agent Manners last night. He told me about Greg Eckman and Linda Baker, the box of goodies, and her proposed trip to China." He glanced at his watch. "Manners was going to confront her this morning and examine the contents of the box. He should be finished by now."

"If Mr. Eckman is in on the smuggling of CRACKERJACK to China, he also has another problem," said Sammy.

"What's that?" asked Phillips.

"A rival company, Thunder Boom Toys, stole the plans for a new computerized toy his engineers developed. We believe it was someone working at Eckman Electronic Toy Factory, someone who had access to the plans." Sammy handed Joyce's list of names to Phillips. "These people had access to the computer files. Checking their bank accounts might reveal any recent large deposits of money."

"You mean payoff money from Thunder Boom Toys," added Phillips.

Sammy nodded.

"It sounds like probable cause to me," said Phillips. "With a warrant I can check out some banks for you." He frowned at the note. "However, I'll need some addresses to go with these names."

"Agent Manners can supply their addresses and probably their social security numbers."

"Did somebody mention my name?" came a voice from the open doorway. Agent Ted Manners squeezed into the room and leaned against the filing cabinet. He looked down at the three teens. "I'm glad you're here. I just came from a talk with

Linda Baker, and I examined the box and its contents." His posture and clothes were professional, but his voice wavered. "CRACKER-JACK wasn't tucked inside the toy or the box. Sammy, it appears you missed an important part of Eckman's conversation with Linda."

Sammy bit his lower lip. "What did I miss?"

"Woo Chung runs a factory in Hong Kong. He manufactures toys for other companies. Three weeks ago he was in our country to drum up business. That's when he paid Eckman a visit. Last week, when Smarty Pants was proven successful, Eckman contacted Linda Baker."

"Why Linda?" asked Joyce.

"They're cousins. Eckman knew that Linda was going on a vacation to China. He asked her to take a working model of Smarty Pants with her to get a price quote from Woo Chung."

"You mean he's thinking of having Smarty Pants made in China?" asked Brian.

"His employees won't like that," said Joyce.

Manners pointed a finger. "That's why Eckman wanted to keep it a secret. If the toy was assembled cheaper in China, he would have to lay off workers here at the factory."

"Does Mr. Eckman or Linda Baker know about CRACKERJACK?" asked Sammy.

"No, I told Linda the FBI was checking out everyone making a trip to China. I didn't tell her why. So when she checks back with Eckman, she'll just say the package was inspected by the FBI."

"So CRACKERJACK is still out there somewhere," said Detective Phillips.

"It's probably in China by now," said Brian, allowing Rubby to take some bunny hops along the edge of the desk.

"Your rabbit seems to be jumpy this morning," said Phillips. "What are you feeding your crime-fighting rabbit?"

"Donuts," said Joyce. "Brian told us he took Rubby into the family restaurant for donuts yesterday."

"I did not," said Brian. "I left Rubby on the bike when I went inside for a donut."

Phillips took another sip of cold coffee. "Maybe that's the trouble. You haven't been feeding him."

Several odd feelings hit Sammy at the same time. He remembered Joyce saying, "Mike. His name is Mike." More feelings generated images. Fragments from the explosion of the images caused the super sleuth to jump up, startling the others in the room.

"What's wrong?" asked the agent.

Sammy stared at Brian. "Brian, are you saying the rabbit was on your bike when you went into the restaurant?"

"Yeah, why?"

"Why wasn't the rabbit stolen with the bike?"

"It was, until I grabbed the handlebars as the boy pushed my bike across the parking lot.

When he kicked me, Rubby unhooked from the brake cables and fell off."

Sammy reached and grabbed the rabbit away from Brian. He turned the animal over and over until he saw the stitches. They formed a line under the fluff on the belly. He squeezed the rabbit several times.

"What are you doing, Sammy?" asked Brian. "It's only a toy. You don't have to give it artificial respiration."

"No, but we may have to perform some surgery," replied Sammy.

Manners and Phillips chuckled, but Joyce knew that Sammy was on to something.

Sammy used his fingers to pull at the stitches. Two big tugs and the stitches pulled loose. Some polyester fiber spilled out. The edge of a small, thin box poked out from the opened seam. He pulled it gently from its hiding place, holding it by the corner.

How ironic, thought Sammy. This time, CRACKERJACK was the prize inside a rabbit. "Here, this might be what you're looking for," he said, handing the small package carefully to Agent Manners.

The code number and warning label on the cover identified its contents. "Code Number CJ210. Attention: contents Static Sensitive. Do not ship or store near strong static, electromagnetic, or radioactive fields."

This time as he spoke, Manners' voice was very professional, very FBI. "Our country can now sleep easier tonight. CRACKERJACK has been recovered."

"See, I told you Rubby would bring us good luck," said Brian. "And there's your proof."

Detective Phillips opened a desk drawer and handed the agent a manila envelope. "If Rubby's luck continues, there'll be fingerprints on the box, and you'll be able to identify your man."

"Thanks," said Manners as he slipped the box inside the envelope. He looked at Brian. "Now, where did you get the rabbit?"

"From the toy factory," said Brian. "Andy Good and Dale Martin gave Joyce and me a dog and that rabbit."

"Where did Good and Martin get them?"

"They're obsolete animals," said Joyce. "They're left over from experiments. They were on a pile with other stuffed toys there on a shelf."

"Where did the stuffed animals come from before that?" asked Manners.

"Inventory. Joseph Sweeney," said Sammy.

Manners shook his head as the familiar list of suspects grew larger. His voice faded. "And before that, from that Shipman guy in Receiving. Well, we have a chain of people who could have slipped CRACKERJACK into the rabbit."

"Plus all the other employees who walked in and out of the department," said Brian.

Ted Manners shook his head. "Hmm, oh, and I have to take the rabbit as part of the evidence."

Sammy handed the rabbit to the agent.

"May I have him back later?" asked Brian. "I don't want to lose my good luck."

"I doubt it, but I'll see what I can do," said Manners. "You kids are incredible. Sammy, how did you know CRACKERJACK was inside the rabbit?"

Sammy knew that his subconscious mind had picked up on clues and fed them to his conscious mind as feelings. His conscious mind then had to translate those feelings into words and images. The young detective found it hard to explain, so he replied, "It's intuition. Sometimes I get certain feelings."

Manners stepped into the doorway. "Well, whatever it is, the FBI could use some of it." He looked back at Phillips. "I have to go and write up my report. I'll check for prints then get back to you." He gave the teens a quick glance. "And, Sammy, if we find no prints, I'll be back. Maybe your intuition can tell us who it is we're looking for."

Under his breath Sammy said, "If you ask me now, I could probably tell you." But it was too late. The agent had already vanished from the hallway.

In Amish Country, all shoulders of the roads were known as buggy lanes. That's not to say that only buggies laid claim to those narrow strips of leftover macadam and dirt. Bicycles, scooters, and skates sometimes joined the sporadic parade of buggies.

Tourists, in their motor trends of the year, slowed down to peer at the Amish, who rode their vintage buggies, scooters, and skates. They shunned the non-Amish bikers, bikers like Sammy Wilson, Brian Helm, and Joyce Myers.

The horse droppings, otherwise known as road apples, were a challenge to the bike riders. It was the price they paid for riding in the buggy lane.

"Hey, watch out!" said Brian. "Another pile is coming up." He swerved his bike around the manure. Helm, Brian Helm, at the moment was a secret road scout. He led the way through the many road hazards, blazing the trail, making the journey safe for his fellow travelers. Secret Agent Helm gladly took on the responsibility of dealing with the dangers that lurked ahead of them in the buggy lane. Soon he had his friends back in the safety of Sammy's house.

"We're not just going to sit around and wait, are we?" asked Brian as he and Joyce sat down at the kitchen table.

Sammy volunteered to feed the amateur detective team. His mother usually stocked the refrigerator with chipped ham, cheese, and Lebanon bologna. In a matter of seconds, the teenagers slapped together their own tailor-made sandwiches and were ready for brainstorming.

"No. We have to do something," said Sammy in answer to Brian's earlier question. "Now that the computer module has been found, we need to prove who was involved. I suggest we don't wait for the fingerprint results as they may turn up nothing."

"The one thing in our favor," said Joyce, "is that nobody at the factory knows the module has been found."

Brian swallowed and added more ham to his sandwich. "I can't believe CRACKERJACK was in Rubby all that time." He shook his sandwich at Sammy. "Okay, how did you know CRACKERJACK was inside my rabbit?"

"Once I factored in the rabbit as the target of the theft, the rest was easy. The stitches on the rabbit were hand-sewn. When I squeezed the rabbit, I could feel something inside. Then when I saw a package, I knew for sure."

"The boy who stole my bike is in on it," said Brian. "Probably related."

"Could be," said Joyce.

Sammy remembered that Brian's rabbit had been taken as evidence. "If we can get our hands on another identical rabbit," said Sammy, "we could flush out the culprit."

"Yeah," said Brian. "We use the rabbit as bait. We place him out in the open, and we hide, and when—" Brian stopped.

Sammy had that look again, the one that announced: Brain cells at work. Caution: Do not talk while the thinking process is in motion. Plan under construction.

Brian and Joyce knew the signs and used the opportunity to finish their sandwiches. The excitement plus having the equivalent of two sandwiches caused Brian to lose his appetite. Joyce finished her milk.

With a glint in his eye and a look of satisfaction, Sammy resumed eating.

The silence tormented Brian. Too many seconds went by. "Well, tell us," said Brian. "What's the plan? You have a plan. Right, Sammy?"

The bright teenager rubbed his hands together, causing the crumbs to land on his paper plate. He leaned back and looked seriously at Brian. "Tomorrow at ten o'clock, we have an appointment to see Mr. Eckman. I'm going to call him today and ask him to check in Inventory for a twelve-inch, gray rabbit. I'm sure they'll have another one there. Brian, you're going to keep the appointment and pick up the rabbit."

Brian waited for more. "Is that it?"

"That's it."

"Oh, I get it," said Brian, jumping up from his chair. "Then the fun begins. Right, Sammy?"

"Brian, you are so right. Then the fun begins."

# *Chapter Sixteen*

Wearing the cautious look of a secret agent, Helm, Brian Helm, double-oh-seven and a half, slunk into the reception area. His suspicions were confirmed. The reception desk was empty. He was alone. Or was he? Beads of sweat formed on his forehead. He quickly rang the bell. That maneuver was in the training manual. *When in the presence of a bell, ring it.*

The bell's loudness caused the teen to spin around, expecting the enemy to attack from the rear. His arms flailed about as he showed off some creative karate moves. When he opened his eyes, no one was there . . . unless the evildoers were invisible. Yes, that was it. They—

Molly suddenly appeared through a side door. Brian's apprehension increased. "The Bride of Frankenstein" had returned. The receptionist had reverted to her archaic look of yesteryear. She wore a dark long dress, dark long hair, a dark long face, and probably dark long johns. "Hello, Brian. You're early. Are you waiting for your friends?"

Brian stood tall with shoulders back. "No, I can handle this by myself," he said with no conviction.

"Have a seat, and I'll tell Greg . . . Mr. Eckman you're here."

Five minutes later, Molly escorted Brian into the office. As she left the two alone, she wondered what the gray rabbit was doing on Greg's desk.

"There's your rabbit," said Eckman. "Sammy said the other one was stolen along with your bike."

"Ah, oh, yeah," stammered Brian. "They took my bike and all."

Eckman picked up the rabbit and threw it at Brian. "You can tell your friends that I'm suing Thunder Boom Toys. If you kids come up with anything, let me know."

Before Brian could respond, the door opened. "They're here," said Molly.

Joseph Sweeney, Marty Shipman, Andy Good, and Dale Martin marched in. They all stared at Brian—and the rabbit.

"You all know Brian Helm," said Eckman.

"Yeah, hi, Brian," said Andy. The others smiled and nodded.

"I called you in here to tell you we've started legal action against Thunder Boom Toys. I just got the call from the lawyer. I wanted you to hear it from me rather than from rumors. I'd appreciate it if you could spread the word around to let the others know."

"Sure, we'll do that," said Shipman. The others nodded in agreement.

Greg Eckman stood. "That's all. You can go back to work."

Sweeney was the last to leave. He took one last look at the rabbit on Brian's lap. It looked like the one Eckman had gotten from him that morning. He shrugged and slowly closed the door.

Eckman shuffled some papers on his desk and then checked Honey, the breakaway dog, to make sure she was all in one piece.

An awkward silence permeated the office.

"I guess I better go," said Brian, rising and keeping a tight grip on the rabbit.

"Brian, before you go, will you do me a favor?" asked Eckman. "Down in the cellar is something I want you to see. It might be worth mentioning in the news article Joyce is writing."

"Sure," said Brian, pleased that this man knew that he was still in the room.

"Look, I have to make an important phone call. Do you mind going by yourself?"

Brian didn't want to hear that. "Well, I don't know. I . . ."

Eckman pointed. "You go down the hall out here. You know where the steps are that go upstairs. Right behind them is the door that leads down to the cellar. The light switch is on the wall inside the door."

The person leaning against the other side of the office door had heard enough. A nervous smile developed. The Watcher had become The Listener. A plan was forming as the figure hurried away in the direction of the cellar door.

Brian didn't exactly feel alone now that he had the rabbit. He strolled down the hall, past the stairway, until he was face to face with the cellar door. His hand rose slowly and turned the knob. Brian shook, the rabbit shook, and the doorknob shook as the door squeaked open. Light reflected from below. Somebody had already switched on the light.

Had Mr. Eckman expected him to visit the cellar? What was he supposed to see? What could be in a cellar of an eighty-year-old building? Eighty years. That's a long time. Ghosts? *No*, thought Brian. *Ghosts don't really exist. Do they?* His eyes darted down to where the steps ended. *Hm, not much light*, thought Brian. *Probably just a storage area.* That's it. Mr. Eckman wanted him to see something that was stored down there. Can ghosts be stored? Monsters? Evil critters?

Brian threw the rabbit so that it bounced on the last two steps and landed on the concrete cellar floor. He was testing the layout of the territory like any responsible secret agent would do. What if monsters tackled and devoured the rabbit? Better the rabbit than himself, he thought. When the rabbit remained in one piece, Brian started down the stairs. He descended slowly—to allow the cellar to adjust itself to his presence.

When he reached the second to last step, he hunched down and peered around. The cellar was one big room with the stairway at one end. Four or five sixty-watt light bulbs were playing a tug-of-war with the darkness. The darkness was winning. The first object Brian saw was a large metal shoe—about size one hundred three. *It must belong to a giant*, thought Brian. He shivered. There's nothing meaner than a giant who lost a shoe.

Several large cardboard boxes and wooden packing crates were stacked against one wall. Each was labeled with its contents. Piles of printed material, paper, and cardboard, acting as a partial room divider, towered to the unfinished ceiling. The huge, black furnace, unused for forty years, sulked in a corner like a dying monster.

Okay, he had seen the cellar. It was time to move on. He was about to rebound up the steps when something moved.

He froze.

Silence.

It moved again. Then . . .

Music.

It moved to the music: a life-size angel decked out in a white gown. White sparkling lace whirled itself around the heavenly creature. The angel glowed, adding dignity and grace to an otherwise common, dingy storage area.

The angel's presence gave Brian the reassurance of protection from harm. He floated down the last two steps, but when his feet touched the cellar floor, the music stopped. The radiance faded as Brian was grabbed from behind, his mouth gagged, and a burlap bag pulled over his head. Strong arms wrapped strips of cloth around his arms and legs, and he was forced to the floor. When the last knot was tied, he heard the cellar speak for the first time.

"Just stay there and you won't get hurt." The voice was rough and disguised. "I'm sorry, but I have to get this back," said the figure as it bent over and retrieved the rabbit from the concrete floor.

Brian knew he would be in more trouble when CRACKERJACK wasn't found in the stuffed animal. He tried to move his arms. If only he could loosen the knot. He didn't have time. He could hear hands assaulting the rabbit.

Fingers searched through the fluffy fur. "Where are the stitches?" asked the voice. Hands squeezed the rabbit. "Where is it?!" the voice yelled. "This isn't the right rabbit! It's not the rabbit!"

With all the rage it could muster, the figure grabbed Brian and pulled him to his feet. He shook the bound teenager. "Tell me! Tell me! Where is it? Where is the computer chip?"

Brian was scared for his life. He wiggled and strained to get loose. Having his head covered didn't make it any easier. If he could only see the knots. He needed to free his arms. He struggled some more and then stopped abruptly. A second voice exploded from his right.

"Okay, that's enough," said the deep voice advancing toward Brian and the figure.

The individual, still in a frenzy, glanced at the oncoming hulk. He released Brian and, like a trapped animal, bolted for the steps. Halfway up, the figure was subdued by two policemen. Handcuffs were applied, and the prisoner was forced to sit on the lower steps.

With the culprit secured, someone grabbed Brian, loosened the cloth binding, and stripped the burlap bag from his head. Brian blinked a couple of times and then focused on a familiar face.

"Are you okay?" asked Sammy.

Brian, mystified, backed up and rested against the cellar wall. He waited until the fuzzy series of events came into focus. Tired and perplexed, he looked at his pal and said, "You did it to me again. Didn't you?"

"Brian, it was because of you that we caught the guilty party," said Sammy, pointing to the steps.

"But I could have been killed," said Brian.

"Not with me around," said Detective Phillips, now standing in front of the captured individual.

Still in a daze, Brian looked from Phillips to the steps. "That's the person who grabbed me and tied me up? That's who had CRACKERJACK?"

The defeated figure, sitting on the steps, was sobbing, his head in his cuffed hands. Dale Martin lifted his head and looked at Brian. "I'm sorry. I wouldn't have hurt you. I just needed to get the chip back."

"You wouldn't have hurt me?" asked Brian, who was now mad. "What about hurting your country?"

"What do you mean, country?" asked Martin, his face shallow and wet with tears.

Sammy noted Martin's genuine look of surprise. "You were going to send a top-secret intelligence decoding module to China. Were you aware of that?"

"No, you're wrong," said the engineer. "It's a computer chip used for speech and animation."

"I believe you've been misled," said Phillips. "How much were they paying you to ship the module to China?"

Martin lowered his head. "Fifty thousand." His face lifted again. "But it was a chip from Argus Solutions in California. They only make chip modules for toys and things like that."

Sammy knew that Dale Martin had no way of knowing about the top-secret modules developed and produced by Argus. "Who approached you with the offer of fifty thousand dollars?"

"A guy named Steve. I was feeling sorry for myself one day. You know, with my father's illness and all. He knew about my father and all the bills to be paid. It sounded all so simple. How scientists all over the world exchanged ideas so everyone benefited. He explained how China with its large population was suffering because certain people in our government didn't want computer hardware and software to go to China."

"So this Steve focused on your domestic problem," said Phillips.

"He compared the suffering people of China with my suffering father. The fifty thousand dollars would pay off the bills that are piling up. Look, I know it was wrong, but I'd do anything for my father. Anything."

"Is that why you also sold out to Thunder Boom Toys?" asked Brian.

"No, I didn't do that," said Martin. "Someone else did. I wouldn't do that."

Sammy wanted to confirm what he already suspected. "Why did you hide the module in the rabbit?"

"I was instructed to put the chip into the toy shipment to China. I arranged to be in the Packing Department when they put the order together. When I was about to slip the boxed chip in with a toy, Mr. Eckman showed up and started talking to me. The chip remained in my pocket. After that, I didn't know what to do. In a panic, I hid the chip in the rabbit that was on the shelf above my desk."

"Then the unexpected happened," said Sammy.

Dale Martin grimaced. "Yes, Andy gave the rabbit to Joyce. I was mad at first until I realized it was the perfect way to get the chip out of here, past the metal detectors."

"That was you in the blue Sentra that followed Joyce home, wasn't it?"

"Yeah, it was my wife's car. How did you know?"

"When Joyce, Brian, and I came to interview you for the newspaper, you asked Joyce what she had named her stuffed dog."

"Yes, I remember."

"But Joyce had been given the stuffed rabbit. You just said so yourself. Brian was given the dog. Only the person who opened Joyce's camera bag and saw the dog knew the rabbit and the dog had been switched."

"So no one was after the film," said Brian. "He wanted the rabbit."

"Right. When Brian mentioned giving the rabbit to his sister, you had to wait until she returned home from visiting her aunt."

"As I was driving past the restaurant," said Martin, "I saw the rabbit. I couldn't believe it. There it was on the bike. People were all around, and I didn't want to be seen near the rabbit or the bike so I paid a boy to take the bike."

"Why didn't you tell the boy to take just the rabbit?" asked Brian. "Why bother with the bike?"

"I told the boy that you were my nephew, and I wanted to teach you a lesson about locking up your bike so it wouldn't be stolen. He agreed to help me for ten dollars."

"And you didn't get the rabbit after all," said Sammy, "because it fell off the bike when Brian interfered."

Martin wiped his hand across his face. "I was getting desperate. When I saw Brian and the rabbit here in the office, I had to act fast." He took a deep breath. "I guess I acted too fast. I didn't see the trap you laid for me." Hopelessness poured from his eyes as he stared at Sammy. "You're smart, really smart. I'm sorry our friendship had to end like this."

Sammy's eyes glanced at the floor then settled again on Martin. With a slight smile he said, "You have some things in your favor. CRACKERJACK was recovered. The mastermind behind the espionage ring used you. If you identify and testify against the man known as Steve, you'll probably receive leniency from the courts."

Martin shook his head. "In the long run, I didn't help my father after all."

"The solution to your problem isn't money," said Sammy. He picked up the remote control Martin had used to activate the mechanical angel. "The solution is over there." Sammy pointed the control and pushed a button.

A brilliant glow filled the cellar, followed by soft music. They all peered at the center of the light. The angel, draped in white, floated forward and smiled. The words were the music and the music was the words.

*"Love and faith I bring to you. Give it back in what you do."*

Tears again filled Dale Martin's eyes as Detective Phillips read him his rights and led him up the steps and out of the toy factory.

# *Chapter Seventeen*

"Did the angel really talk?" asked Agent Manners.

Brian nodded. "Yeah, you should have been there."

"It sounds like I missed out on something special," said Manners. "Sorry I couldn't be there for the arrest."

"Yeah, me, too," added Joyce.

Sammy, Brian, and Joyce, along with Detective Phillips, John Moore, and Ted Manners, were seated at a table at the Bird-in-Hand Restaurant. Two days had passed since the arrest of Dale Martin. It was at Agent Manners' request that they had gathered for a final get-together. They had already ordered their food.

Joyce reached over to the rabbit on Brian's lap and wiggled its ear. "Brian, that was brave of you, acting as a decoy. You took the rabbit, opened the cellar door, and faced danger head on."

Brian looked at Sammy, who only shrugged.

"Well, I . . . er . . . ah, I threw the rabbit down the steps to alert whoever was there that I was on the way. Then I went down to face—what I had to face. That's when Mr. Martin put the bag over my head and tied me up. That was all part of the plan. Right, Sammy?"

"As it turned out, it's great that you continued with the investigation," said Manners. "We found no fingerprints on the box, and we would have been at a loss to identify anyone."

"When I called Mr. Eckman and explained my plan," said Sammy, "he agreed to help. I suspected Mr. Martin was the man we were looking for, but I couldn't prove it. I arranged with Mr. Eckman to have the suspects in his office to see Brian with the rabbit. I figured the guilty person would make an attempt to snatch the rabbit, thinking the packaged module was still inside. Then Mr. Eckman was to make up an excuse for Brian to visit the cellar."

"Of course Sammy and I were already in the cellar hidden behind some wooden crates," said Phillips. "We saw the lights go on and saw Martin sneak down the steps. Then we heard noise in the back of the stairway area. As it turned out, Martin was looking for something to use to subdue Brian."

Brian plopped his hand on his head. "I'm glad he found the burlap and not a two-by-four."

Phillips twitched his thin mustache. "Has Dale Martin been able to identify this Steve fellow from Argus Solutions?"

"Yes," said the agent. "He looked through hundreds of photos of the employees and others associated with Argus Solutions. He picked out a Steve Willows, who is a supervisor there. It looks like the case is all but closed." The agent waved his hand across from left to right. "That's why I invited you here to the restaurant. I wanted to thank you all personally for your outstanding contributions to this case. It's unbelievable what you three teenagers have done for your country."

Brian sat up, waiting for the medal to be hung around his neck.

Manners glanced at Detective Phillips. "And that goes for the police department, as well." He looked at his good friend, John Moore, and smiled. "And a special thanks to John and his teddy bear, Bigmoore."

John sat back in his chair and allowed the waitress to set a carafe of coffee on the table. She returned with cold drinks for the amateur detectives.

"It's too bad Julia Greenleaf couldn't be here," said John, thinking of the sacrifice she made by stuffing herself into the bear.

"I called to invite her," said Manners, "but I was told she was on vacation."

"You know, Sammy, that's what we need to do—go on vacation, said Brian. "We could spend another fun week at the toy factory." Brian sported a silly grin.

"Which reminds me, Sammy," said Detective Phillips. "I didn't find anything unusual when I checked out the bank accounts."

"And you checked every name on the list?" asked Joyce.

"Yep. Maybe Thunder Boom Toys had an outside man come in and steal the plans to Smarty Pants. Industrial espionage is high-tech these days."

Sammy didn't need to have Phillips repeat what he had just said. He knew the feelings and the images that were flashing in his mind. And it made sense. Sammy slowly raised a finger in the air. "There's one name that's not on Joyce's list."

"Who's that?" asked Brian.

"The one person who had the knowledge, the time, and access to the factory's computer—Julia Greenleaf."

Agent Manners' eyes opened wide. He shook his head. "No, she . . ."

Sammy interrupted. "When we first met you in John's office, Brian mentioned Smarty Pants. Julia was the only person who smiled. She knew what Brian was referring to. Which means she had entered the Smarty Pants computer program. Did Julia have any money when you hired her to help you with this case?"

"No, but . . ."

"Do you know where she is right now?"

"I was told she was on a two-weeks' vacation in Europe."

Sammy leaned closer. "Could she afford that vacation on the money the FBI paid her?"

Ted Manners snickered. "I doubt it."

The super sleuth continued, "Julia wasn't authorized to open any other computer programs except employees' records, sales, and shipping. It will be easy to check the computer to see if Project: Smarty Pants was accessed at the time Julia was there.

"Sammy, this is one time I hope you're wrong," said Manners. "She seemed like a nice person, trying to turn her life around. But, I have a feeling you're right."

"Temptation is stronger when you're poor," said Sammy sadly.

"That just about closes the Case of the Toy Factory," said Brian. "Are we going back to the factory tomorrow?"

Joyce poked Brian's shoulder. "Why? Do you want another free stuffed animal?"

Brian playfully shook the rabbit in Joyce's face. "No, I already have another Rubby." He then petted the rabbit sideways.

"Oh, oh, look out," said Sammy. "Brian's generating good luck."

"Your meal is ready," said the waitress as she arrived with a tray full of food.

Everyone looked in surprise at Brian and the rabbit.

Brian smiled back and rubbed the rabbit a second time.

They waited for something to happen again as the waitress served the food.

When it didn't, Joyce raised her hands, palms up. "Well, where's your second good luck, Brian?"

"Oh, that comes after the dinner," said Brian, starting to eat.

"What do you mean?" asked Agent Manners.

Brian swallowed and smiled. "That's when you pay for our meal."

# Sammy and Brian Mystery Series

#1 **The Quilted Message** by Ken Munro
The whole village was talking about it. Did the Amish quilt contain more than just twenty mysterious cloth pictures? The pressure was on for Bird-in-Hand's two teenage detectives, Sammy and Brian, to solve the mystery. Was Amos King murdered because of the quilt? Who broke into the country store? It was time for Sammy and Brian to unmask the intruder. .......... $4.95

#2 **Bird in the Hand** by Ken Munro
When arson is suspected on an Amish farm, the village of Bird-in-Hand responds with a fund-raiser. The appearance of a mysterious tattooed man starts a series of events that ends in murder. And who is The Bird? Sammy and Brian are bound hand and foot by the feathered creature. Bird-in-Hand's own teenage sleuths break free and unravel the mystery. ..... $5.95

#3 **Amish Justice** by Ken Munro
The duo turns into a trio when Joyce Myers becomes the newest member of the Sammy and Brian detective team. Is farmland in Lancaster County worth killing for? Frank Crawford thinks so. And when the police call the attempts on his life accidents, the old farmer sends for the teenage detectives. The three sleuths soon discover one of five suspects knows about the "IT" under the house. .......... $5.95

#4 **Jonathan's Journal** by Ken Munro
After Scott Boyer comes to town, a young girl disappears. He then makes an offer Sammy and Brian can't refuse. A 200-year-old journal holds a challenge of a lifetime. It holds two secrets: a mysterious puzzle and murder. Bird-in-Hand's super detectives investigate the meaning behind its cryptic message. .......... $5.95

#5 **Doom Buggy** by Ken Munro
An Amish buggy disappears. Twenty cut-out letters appear in its place. Then someone wants George Brock dead—in his welding shop. Sammy, Brian, and Joyce, fifteen-year-old sleuths from Bird-in-Hand, try to find the connection between these three mysterious happenings. .......... $5.95

#6 **Fright Train** by Ken Munro
The actor, John Davenport, retires in Strasburg. He brings with him Manaus, the monster from his cult movie, *Fright Train.* While riding the Strasburg Railroad, Sammy and Brian learn that someone wants to steal something from the actor. But what? Is it his autobiography manuscript? Or is it the "Fright Train"? .................................................. $5.95

#7 **Creep Frog** by Ken Munro
Where in Kitchen Kettle Village is Charles Parker? The frog isn't talking, but Zulu, the African parrot, has plenty to say. Charles Parker is masquerading under a new identity in Kitchen Kettle Village. U.S. Marshals want Sammy and Brian to find their hidden witness before Mack Roni, a thug, finds him. The frog is kidnapped, but why? And—will someone kiss the frog and turn him into Charles Parker? .................................. $5.95

#8 **The Number Game** by Ken Munro
Sidney Thomas, being chased by the police, has to make a hasty decision. Where can he hide a million dollars in diamonds at Root's Country Market? The mystery starts at the Conestoga Auction. Does the painting or the vase hold the secret to the diamonds? Joyce Myers joins Sammy and Brian in search of a briefcase full of diamonds. And—who is the masked man? .................................................. $5.95

#9 **The Tin Box** by Ken Munro
After Sammy and Brian find a tin box buried in a cellar wall, five people from North Carolina arrive in Bird-in-Hand. They're all looking for Shawn Walker. One of "The North Carolina Five" doesn't want him found. A note from Shawn Walker takes the amateur detectives to Borders and Barnes and Noble. Can the super sleuths "sting" a blackmailer? And—who is Henry Schnobel, the Third? .................................................. $5.95

- - - - - - - - - - - - - - - - - - - - - - -

These books may be purchased at your local bookstore or ordered from Gaslight Publishers, P. O. Box 258, Bird-in-Hand, PA 17505. Enclosed is $__________ (please add $2.00 for shipping and handling). Send check or money order only.

Name ______________________________________________

Address ____________________________________________

City ____________________ State _________ Zip Code ___________